rev 9/2015

X

BOOKS BY JOHN CAGE

EMPTY WORDS

M
Writings '67– '72

SILENCE
Lectures and Writings

A YEAR FROM MONDAY
New Lectures and Writings

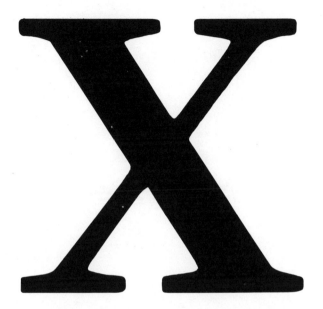

WRITINGS '79–'82

WESLEYAN UNIVERSITY PRESS

Middletown, Connecticut

Most of the works in this volume have previously appeared elsewhere:

The first part, including the preface, of "James Joyce, Marcel Duchamp, Erik Satie: An Alphabet" appeared in *Zero* in 1981.

"Another Song" appeared in 1981 in *Another Song*, Callaway Editions, New York.

"B.W. 1916–1979" was published in the *Proceedings of the American Academy of Arts and Letters* in 1980.

"Composition in Retrospect" was published by Point Publications in 1982.

Mesostics:

"There is not much difference between the two" appeared in *Misuzi 1979*, Tokyo.

"Toyama 1982" was published by the Museum of Modern Art, Toyama, Japan, in 1982.

"Untitled" appeared in the United States in *Chelsea* in 1980.

"for her first exhibition with love" appeared in an exhibition catalog, FANNY "nach Straßburg" Collagen 1980–82, Frankfort/Main, in 1982.

Permissions:

The original text on which "Writing for the Fourth Time through Finnegans Wake" and "Muoyce (Writing for the Fifth Time through Finnegans Wake)" are based is *Finnegans Wake* by James Joyce, © 1939 by James Joyce. © renewed 1967 by George Joyce and Lucia Joyce. This text is used by kind permission of the Society of Authors, London.

From *The Bride Stripped Bare By Her Bachelors, Even* by Marcel Duchamp, used by permission of Richard Hamilton.

From *A L'infinitif* by Marcel Duchamp, used by permission of A.H. Ekstrom.

Écrits by Erik Satie (collected by Ornella Volta), used by permission of M. Joseph Lafosse–Satie.

From *The Cantos of Ezra Pound*, copyright © 1969 by Ezra Pound, and from Cantos LXXII and LXXIII, copyright © 1973 by the Trustees of the Ezra Pound Literary Property Trust, used by permission of New Directions Publishing Corporation.

All inquiries and permissions requests should be addressed to the Publisher, Wesleyan University Press, 110 Mt. Vernon Street, Middletown, Connecticut 06457

Distributed by Harper & Row Publishers, Keystone Industrial Park, Scranton, Pennsylvania 18512

Library of Congress Cataloging in Publication Data
Cage, John.
  X.
  I. Title.
PS3553.A32X2 1983   818'.5407   83-18275
ISBN 0-8195-5090-6

Manufactured in the United States of America
First Edition

In Memory of Bill Bueno (Jose Rollin de la Torre Bueno)
1904–1980
Editor for the Wesleyan University Press
1958–1979

CONTENTS

FOREWORD

I am as ever beholden to R. Buckminster Fuller. His recent books *Critical Path* and *Grunch of Giants* clearly tell what our world situation is and what must be done if life on earth is to continue. Though some nations have tried, none has succeeded in becoming supranational. Only business, industry, most of it American, Coca-Cola, for instance, is downright global in its operation.

Nations belong to the past. They merely fight one another. We must study carefully the ways of large industry, so that we can implement the fact that there is no limit to the place in which we live. Patriotism? Take it with you out into space!

National differences can be dissolved by global problems. If we were to be attacked from outer space we would all quickly get together. Industry is now beginning to suggest that the differences between currencies should be eliminated. It would simplify the counting of profits.

The title of this book, like that of *M*, was found by subjecting the alphabet to chance operations. It signifies the unknown, place where poetry lives, tomorrow, I hope, as it does today, where what you see, framed or unframed, is art (cf. photography), where what you hear on or off the record is music.

Years ago in a review of *Silence* Alfred Frankenstein wrote that my writings were the story of how a change of mind came about. From the beginning in the late '30s I have been more interested in exemplification than in explanation, and so I have more and more written my texts in the same way I write my music, and make my prints, through the use of chance operations and by taking the asking of questions rather than the making of choices as my personal responsibility. Or you might say that I am devoted to freeing my writing from my intentions, and so, in those cases like the writings through Joyce's *Finnegans Wake* and *The Cantos* of Ezra Pound included in this book in which chance plays no part, I merely follow the rolling of a metal ball (the name of the author through his work) which serves to free me and the reader not only of my intentions but also of those of Joyce and Pound. I am confident, however, and some friends support this view, that Joyce would have been delighted by what happens when intention is removed from the *Wake,* and I hazard that Pound, if not delighted, would have been relieved. *Canto CXX:* "Let those I love try to forgive what I have made."

X, then, as I write in the *Diary* (CCXXIV, 6th remark), is one book, the most recent, in an ongoing series: to find a way of writing which comes from ideas, is not about them, but which produces them.

It is illustrated fortuitously by twelve color photographs made at my request by Paul Barton of twelve weathered images on the Siegel Cooper Building, first balcony level (eight images on the Avenue of the Americas, two on 18th Street, two on 19th Street, New York City). I call them *Weather-ed I-XII.* I did nothing to make them the way they are. I merely noticed them. They are changing, as are the sounds of the traffic I also enjoy as each day I look out the window.

In January 1979, Louis Mink wrote me an excellent letter saying that having been reading my first *Writing* he noticed that I had invented the impure mesostic. A pure mesostic, he said, would not permit the appearance of either letter between two of the name. This criticism fascinated me and I profited from it by writing a third time through *Finnegans Wake*. That text resembles the first, whereas the following fourth *Writing*, which follows the same rule, like the second does not permit the reappearance of a given syllable for a given letter of the name. It is the shortest of the four writings.

WRITING FOR THE FOURTH TIME THROUGH FINNEGANS WAKE

I

wroth with twone nathandJoe   3
A
Malt
jhEm
Shen

pftJschute
Of finnegan
that the humptYhillhead of humself
is at the knoCk out
in thE park

Jiccup   4
the fAther
My shining
thE
Soft

Judges
Or helviticus
sternelY
watsCh
futurE of his

Jebel
And
heed   it May half
havE
hiS back   5

and the derryJellybies   6
arOund
fancYmud
ereCtion
dimb   hE

fJord
his bAywinds'
hiM
hEr   7
innS

Jamey
Our   8
paddY
is a ffrinCh tip this is
bullEt that byng

mons inJun   this is the
Alps hooping to
sheltershock the three lipoleuMs
with thEir
book of Stralegy

Jinnies is a
willingdOne
phillippY   9
dispatCh
to irrigatE

                    Jinnies
                 to fontAnnoy
            bode belchuM
                 bonnEt
                 to buSby

            waxing ranJymad   10
                    fOr
                   hneY
                    Cry
            willingdonE

                    Jig-
                 lAnthern
                 Month
            and onE
                 and Such

                    Jist   11
                   dOes
            till bYes will be
                   fliCk
                      flEckflinging its pixylighting

                 Job of   12
                 bAndy
                 Mounds
                 likE
                   So

                 muJikal   13
                  bOx
                 mirY
                  inCabus
                 usEd

mammon luJius
in his grAnd old
historioruM
wrotE
annalS f.

up Jerrybuilding   1 5
tO the
Year
aCross
us frEsh

Junipery
or Alebrill
Mahan   it is   16
wE
kraalS

Jute
let us swOp hats
Yutah
hasatenCy
i trumplE

i rimimirim   Jute
one eyegonblAck
ghinees hies good for you   Mutt
how woodEn i not know
old grilSy

Just   17
hOw
bY a riverpool
Clompturf
rEx

4

              of obJects   19
                Alfrids
              corMacks and
                arE
                  See

                  Jadesses with
                mOuths   and
                saY too us
                niCk
        sons littlEsons

                  Jined   20
                mAy his
                  Mud
              sundEr
              it cloSeth

                  Jarl van   21
              lamphOuse
                  laYing
                  Cold hands
        on himsElf   and his

                  Jiminies cousins of
                cAstle
              derMot
        prankquEan
                a roSy one

        up the Jiminy
          with sOft
                mY earin stop
              to tauCh him his
                  shE

Just
doAt with his
postMan's knock round
his oldE
lauS

Jane's a
cOming
theY're sure
a tourCh of
flamE

no Jugglywuggly
with her wAr souvenir
Murial
assurE
a Sure there

maJesty
who wAs or often feigned to be
froM
inquirE what
had cauSed

Jubilee
drOgheda
sYmbolising puritas
doCtrina
businEss

Jointly kem
the quiet dArkenings of
Mr
aftEr
callouS

Jesuit's
clOth
Yet in
the faCts was
sEcondary

Jenny
eglAndine's choicest
housingrooM
abidE with
my horSe delayed nom num the

many Jiffies
pOtlids
theY
Curiously
thosE

Joined
Apply
toMorrow casual and a
variEty
juSt been

Juiced after
Over at
tarrY the
Clings
hEr

John   61
leAned
Moult
instEnch of
gladSome

heJirite   62
silentiOussuemeant under
deep Your
luCtuous
pEasant

Jink ghostly
As were he
to condeMn
so thEy might
him firSt pharoah

Jumphet   64
frOm
plaYing
on the raglar roCk to dulyn
prisEd

astrollaJerries
for the love of the sAunces
Machinsky
or othEr
muSclebound from being too pulled

a large Jugful   65
sOmeplace
slY where
he Could
mixErs

Joking
lAying if
coMpanion who stuck still to
invEntion
Strongbox

J.   83
befOre
gaY
whiskwigs wiCk's
Ears

Jennerously exhibited   84
to the pArts
it proved Most
fortunatE that
and Six

whole padderJagmartin   86
cOpperas
chrYstalisations of alum on even
to stiCk
firE to

Jew's totems tospite of the
scAttery kind when
Mains
atE
Selling the gentleman

gale and roaring o'crian Jr.   87
bOth
dalkeYs kings of mud and
Crimson
o'donnEr   ay

                    Jowl   89
            the mAthers of
        hircuM
            answEr
                    Siar i am

                    it Jah   90
            i shOuld
                    Yes
        how suCh
                    bEginall finally struck him now

                punic Judgeship
        strove with penAl
                stucckoMuck   91
                    fEw
                jurorS

            and highaJinks   94
                    nOw
            minster York   do i mind   i mind the   95
                rossies Chaffing him
    you do todo north mistEr

                        Jonnies
            hold hArd
                    i'M glad
                    sEz
            lankyShield   gobugga ye

                Jackass   harik   harik   96
            the rOse is white in the
                    rhYme   and
                    Contradrinking
                ninE

Juletide's   97
geniAl
Mullinahob
thEn
upon tankardStown the outlier

the Jenny infanted the
hOux
awaY   98
a dutCh bottom tank
undEr

asia maJor
flAtty
of his oMnibox
hE
almS of

Jams
tOwards
he and Yew
evereaChbird   from golddawn   99
glory to glowworm glEam

Jest
rAce
fieldMarshal
princE
with a moliamordhar manSion in the

Jutstiff   100
buttertOwer
the wasting wYvern
baCkwords
or morE strictly

iuld van diJke
           certAin fixed residents
through our systeM
           bE
           Still o

           Jeer and   101
zhanyzhOnies
had given his eYe for her bed
and a tooth for a Child
           till onE

           Journey to   104
   never hAs
with the cooMbing of
       of aEgypt
       wiSh i

       my o'Jerusalem   105
and i'm his pO
       train trY
       he Can
       Explain

   what Jumbo
       mAde to
       Mouth
   stoppEd
       Should flow and

maJesty
bOrn
uggamYg hapaxle
Country
stilEs

for the grApe vine
ruM
his End for him
off Sooth

diapered windOw
baYleaves
nondesCript
a palmtailEd

final always Jims
sAhib
exhibitionisM
of thosE
capriciouS

amOng
as daY the
loCks
you'rE

first instAnt
nor the huMphar
still kEpt
Small

and looJing
   tOrba's
   aY and would have as true as
muCh
   onE's half

   Jhon   126
rAted
Mic
   thEm and
artful diSorder

   Jaypees and   134
theban recensOrs
   the maYds was midst the hawthorns   135
   pimploCo
to stand for suE

   on a fJeld duiv   136
ruz the hAlo
on the lodge for hyMn
   dapifEr
   magnuS

   Juts   138
he's cOme
shampaYing
   Clouts and
pottlEd

                    Jorn   142
                    bArty
                and toM
        8 and how war yorE
                    anSwer

                    Jeff's   143
                    gOt the signs
                but Yurning
                lovemutCh
                    a brEf burning till

                    Jumps   145
            so she sAys
                so Mush
            not takE it
                courSe i know

                    Jump
                    yOur
                    trYsting   146
                    buCking
                    hopE in

        gilda hilda ita Jess   147
                    kAtty lou
                reforMatory
            pravidancE
                    waS

                    Javanese i will give all my   152
                    Old
                    hYbreds and
            harped on his Crown and
        out of his immobilE

                                            19

Juice of   153
hAd
Must to
hic sor a stonE
Singularly illud

kelkefoJe funcktas   160
kelkefOje
crYing to
reCoil
with a grEat

sotisfiction how his abJect   161
is nothing so much more thAn
the dogMarks
of origEn on
Same time and with the

Jaw   162
mOuthful   163
butYrum
ut sCiat
malum Et

Jeffet   168
four-in-hAnd
buM and dingo jack by
brokE
to Say

Jem is   169
Are
sheM's
gEtup it
Skull an eight of a

tragic Jester   171
sObbed himself
Yellagreen funkleblue windigut
applejaCk
to hEar him twixt his

Johns is   172
next plAce
for luvvoMony
hopEd or at
among morticianS

Jansens chrest   173
wOuld
samtalaisY
merChant
bElfry

and Judder on the mound   175
heAth
heMpal
poursuivE
frownS

in Junk et sampam   178
his bOnafide
straY whizzer sang out
to avenge maC
jobbEr

                    Jymes   181
        wishes to heAr
                    druMcondriac
                    rEally
                    Shamiana   182

                    obJects   183
        cast at gOblins
                    Young
                        Clippings from
        toothsomE

                    Jos   184
                    giAs neys
            the stoMach
        fair chancE of
            tumult Son of

                    Jigsmith
                    dOdginess
        whites and Yolks and
                    Cinnamon
        and asthEr's mess and

                    Joyntstone   192
        let him pAss
        with your cruMbs   193
                    tEll me
        not a loanShark   look

                    Jigs and
                    innOcence   194
                        we Yield our spiritus to the wind
        the pole the spaniel paCk
                        thEir quarry

piped und ubanJees twanged with
rOtundarkinking
nYne   206
tell me quiCk and dongu
maguE

Join in the
gigguels   i cAn't
by the holy well of Mulhuddart
swEar i'd
killy'S mount

and a Jetty amulet   207
clicking cObbles and
eY
annushka lutetiavitCh pufflovah
lEllipos

of inJons
hold your peAce and listen well
it Might
tEn
allcloSe or the nexth of

Jary   210
saccO
and llewelYn mmarriage a brazen nose
Craig and a
harE

Jones
loAf of
Morning for
valE
and outflaSh

                    Jill   211
                  brOth
                  tYne
                  viCtor
                rakE and

                    Joys
                  sAint
                  Moor
                sawyEr and
            tropical Scott

                    Jane in decline and my   214
                  mOngrel
                laundrYman
                    Collars and
                  hEir

                    II

opal who having Jilted   220
                  seAn
                      geMinally about caps or puds
              a pattErn
                      Set and brought home

                    Jibsheets and
              supercargO
            gugnir his geYswerks   221
            his earsequaCk
                  milldiEuw and butt of

                    Jests
            for the wAke lent
                  M.
                finnEgan
            hairwigS

                    and Jean   222
                        sOuslevin bass
                    claYblade
                    of Clubs   to part from
                    fEar   acts of

                    dJowl
              releAsed
        shehind hiMs back
                    unhErd of   223
        mary louiSan

                    Jawr
              in the frOnt
                 givin Yoe   up
        with searCh a fling
              did diE

                    an inJine ruber   224
                    At his thinker's
freightfullness whoM
              his collinE born
                    She

                    ploung Jamn   225
                    sO
                        Yateman hat
              stuCk hits
        althrough his spokEs and if

                    would Jused sit it   229
                    rAte in blotch
              in hyMns
        ignorancE
                    Sorey

worth leaving   neJ   230
             zOkrahsing
pumme if Yell
       while itCh ish   231
       shomE

             by Jove chronides seed
summ After
             Malthos
       rollEd
             Snivelled

             Jerk
a redhOt turnspite
       whY was that
his spurt of Coal   232
       dilutE

             Juwells   236
       fAns
       foMor's in his
paaralonE
dublin'S all adin

       theJ
       thOu
       straYed
of pa's teapuCs
       as lithE and

             Juneses   238
duel mAkes their triel   eer's
       coMbs
       honEy
       yourSelf

her eckcot hJem   242
his flamen vestacOat
      ˙Yahrds of annams   243
    Call
wrongEd by

      Jempson's weed decks   245
bong   bAngbong
  how Matt your
    lukEd your
     mugS and troublebedded

     biJ de   -246
    whO
  fifteen Years
    ·Campus
   thEm

    Jerkoff
   eAtsoup
  yeM or
worth hEaling
   muSt walk out   and

    Jasper and   249
   fOndance and
curtseY one
mettenChough
   thEy

    Jocubus   nic for   251
  stAnth
   Mun in his
sonsEpun
  wiSe

aux Jours des
trAnslout
Mail so
cowriE card i
Sad

hooJahs   282
dOwn
Yerthere
unn enoCh   283
Endso

Joke   290
will hAve
synchronisMs all
quatrEn
whoSe

in par Jure il
Other
Yves   291
so inseuladed as Crampton's
Eurn

Jup   294
cArpenger
centruM and olaf's
cyclonE
aS

Jukes   295
private prOperties
the Yules
sundaClouths
hung up for tatE and comyng

Jeldy   297
this is whAt you'll
            Mygh and thy
spit of dEad
      diScinct

            armJaws at the   300
de vere fOster
        sprY him   301
      miCk
      varsEs

      apoloJigs   302
        thAnks
      leMan
jow low jurE
plumpduffS

      aJax   306
fire at the sOuth
            sYstem   thc uses
and abuses of inseCts
            pEnny post   307

            Jomsborg   310
tuned up by twintriodic singulvAlvulous
        tyMpan
      rEunion
      aSkold

till time Jings
hOst
the keY of efas-taem o   311
a ketCh or hook
alivE a suit

Jewr of   312
plebs but plAbs by low
Mint   313
liquid couragE
Stowed

apullaʃibed the   317
pOwer
Yon peak
with its Coast so
knEw

Jelks   let be buttercup   321
bAll
you scuM   322
turnEd out
alaS

lavantaʃ   325
ahOrace
Ysnod
sCat
doEs

Jodhpur   329
smAlls
i. Magnus
good lifEbark
onSlought

                        Juinnesses   333
rapin his hind   and the bullingdOng
                        staYs outsize her
                        blanCking
                    dronnings kissEd

                        Jude   if you'll   334
                    stAy where you're
                    Mizzatint
                canins to ridE with
                    caninS that lept

                    aJaculate   338
                the glOwrings
                    bruYant the bref
                sing Ching
                    lEw mang

                    Jupes   339
                grAze the
                consoMation
                rEnt
                S

                the dJublian   340
                trulOck
                nYe
            to reguleCt
            stragglEs for

                his muJiksy's
                fArst
            which seeMs   341
            to sharpnEl
                    Spool of the little brown

Jiff exby 369
rOde
the rhYmer that lapped at the hoose
Court
sEight of that yard

Joynes 370
trAynor
to puMp
firE
into thoSe

Jameseslane   begetting a wife 373
which begame his niece by pOuring her
dizzY
Crops out
in your flEsh 374

that Juke built 375
wAit till they send you to
woMhoods   two
twElfth
gaSping

of a rhutian Jhanaral
widOwer
me prhYse
Caulking
any shapE

and a good Jump powell 376
cleAn over
the Massus for to
barrEl
Slick

Jitters   377
          yOu'll
               Yores the strake of
     the Cloth
     to forE of

     so hattaJocky only   383
               quArtebuck   384
          interiMs
for auld lang synE
          palmS in their

               Jules   386
     with the hOughers
               Yaman
     from the Curragh and   387
and the authoritiEs noord

               Jib
               hAirshirt
               reMinds
          villEm and
     blank printS

     of lady Jales casemate
          the fOurth
          raYburn
     the old Conk   -388
          yE gink

III

Joust   416
tAntoo
o Moy
hEartily
Swallowed the

Jiltses   417
gracehOper
in the mYre
aCtually
and preEsumptuably sinctifying

Jetty   420
noon sick pAson
opened by Miss
nighumplEdan
Shout at

contempt and deJeunerate   422
a skillytOn be thinking
i buY him
halfCousin
of minE pigdish   nor wants to

Jeune premier   430
fAirest done
sMilingly
broad by brEad and
Slender

Jaun asking kindlily
hillO missies after their
tYke   431
benediCt
world and his lifE

Jomping   441
hAul
libidinuM in
you'vE
thingS to look

our Jakeline sisters   447
Out
like hYmn
their Coals
will soothE

Jno
egAn
for freedoM of   448
uproosE
of lorcanSby

crekking Jugs at   449
grenOulls
in the shY orient   450
poaCh
rEnt

Jiesis
in the lAtcher
suMtotal
wholE   451
Strafe

                    to Jeshuam i'm   452
                    nOrawain
                        Yous to be   453
        sweeping reduCtions
                    wEaring out your

                        June to our snug   454
                    rewArd
                        luMp it   455
                but givE it
                    flock'S at home

                for the Jemes   456
                        Oh
                chutneY and
                    naboC and
                    fustfEd

                        Jooks
                    the Act
        him   i'll stuMp it out of
                doorstEp
                        Saint   457

                        Jungfraud's   460
                    pOsts
                        waYs and her
                    twiCk
                twinklE twings my twilight

                        Jill   462
                his fAil
                    sMall
                    placE
                        i Smelt the

phopho   foorchtha   aggala   Jeeshee   475
                                      clAss of
                                      Making
                              squarE
                              yardS of him one half

                                    oh Jeyses fluid   480
                            it's his lOst chance
                            heY   did
                    own tripe aCushla
                    that you tiEd

                                    Jong   482
                            of mAho
                            of the Mghtwg grwpp is
                            your wEight
                            hooShin

                    ho look at my Jailbrand   484
                              exquOvis and
                    angliceY
                                    suCk at   485
                    whosE was

                              dJoytsch
            oy soy bleseyblAsey where to go
            is knowing reMain
                    discoursE
                              uS

                              of Jenkins'
                    dullaphOne
                    anglY mo
              moohootCh
              nipponnippErs   -486

Juts   491
luckchAnge
deMaasch
strikE
drarakS

dJanaral when he was sitting him   492
vOlvular with
vikramaditYationists   493
mendaCiis
yErds and

Jorth would come   496
bumgAlowre
seeMly
hEavy
in Sugar

Jusse   502
icecOld
plaYs
one expeCts that kind of
rimEy

Joints   503
cAused
siMply
wEllknown
winning'S

Jazzlike   511
brOllies
beYawnd
tweendeCks
shubladEy's

Jokes bowlderblow the   517
mAsket off
sMutt
dykE
　　Shine

the muJic   518
peace   *in vOina*
　　if You've   519
pootsCh
and proprEy

Juppettes   531
gAuse be
hobMop
shakE up
　　Sake   all

Jaunted   542
rapt in necklOth and sashes
　while the Yanks   543
　were huCkling
　　pEtitions full of

Jets   548
wAterroses
piM's and
pyrrhinE
　　Sourire

their Juremembers 557
imputAtions of
Mitigation
in any casE
waShleather

Jark 558
vOlans at six
Yeastwind and the hoppinghail
outskirts of City 559
groovE two

Jezebel 562
in mAidenly
Much
dulcE
onSk   a lovely

Jem 563
will knOw him
lYlian and
bredsCrums
jEskoff and

Juices 564
olAve
tonoblooM
bluE
markS athwart

gaiJ 565
vOrtigern
muY
malinChily
fathEr

Joustle for   568
but mArk
pouM
pEal
our boorgomaiSter thon

maJers   arise sir
hOrse
alfi bYrni gamman dealter
eaCla
trEacla youghta

Juin   569
shAll
Marlborough-
protEctor
Shall have open

hedJes   571
sOld
i praY
horsehem Coughs
a noisE

conJunct   573
consummAte
Mauritius with sulla
translatE a
goodS of cape

Jumped   578
she's bOrrid his head under
konYglik shire with his
duCk-on-   579
wEnt up

stands abJourned 585
  is lArgely
    Misturbing your nighboor
  tirEd
    Strictly

    Jeebies ugh 590
  yOnd
christmastYde easteredman   fourth
    sCalp halp
  drummEd all

IV

  by Joge 594
you've tippertAps in your
      exMooth ostbys 595
    Each and
  dombS

he conJured himself
thetheatrOn 596
  chYst
  repurChasing his
  sorEnsplit and

    Jerks 611
the rApe
  huMp 612
    Ebblybally
    Sukkot punc

hugly Judsys what 620
  mOre matcher's
sluskY
  teaChing
  mE

              our Joornee   621
              mAke it
              Mrknrk
          your grEat
    languo of flowS

              Jumpst   626
             thrObbst
               Yed
           me Coolly
    and i'd liE as

"THERE IS NOT MUCH DIFFERENCE BETWEEN THE TWO." (SUZUKI DAISETZ)

                  iT
              is A long time
          i don't Know how long
                sInce
    we were in a room toGether   now i hear
              that yoU are dead   but whcn i think of
    you as now i have the Clear impression
                  tHat
          tenderly smIling you're alive as ever

TOYAMA 1982

              deaTh is
                At all times
                liKe
                lIfe
      now that you are a Ghost
                  yoU are as you were
                  a Center among centers
            world-Honored
          world-honorIng

            late yeSterday evening
                tHe moon in los angeles
      low in the east   not fUll
            do you see suZuki daisetz
            give him my lOve

The title of this lecture is a reference to the poetry of Jackson Mac Low, which I have enjoyed for at least twenty-five years. He has made many "Vocabularies," restricting each to the letters to be found in the name of a particular friend. It is possible to imagine that the artists whose work we live with constitute not a vocabulary but an alphabet by means of which we spell our lives. This idea as a subject interests me but it is not what I have done in the following text, though the works of Joyce, Duchamp, and Satie in different ways have resisted the march of understanding and so are as fresh now as when they first were made. I don't know how many books on *Hamlet* there are that set out to elucidate its mysteries, but there begin to be a very large number in relation to the work of Joyce and the work of Duchamp. I prefer the ones that pay attention but stop short of explanation. I enjoy the writing of Anne d'Harnoncourt and Kynaston McShine about Duchamp and that of Adaline Glasheen and Louis Mink about Joyce. When it comes to Satie, I prefer Satie himself to all those who've written about him. The Japanese composer and pianist Yuji Takahashi told me he liked two kinds of music, that that had too many notes and that that had too few. His remark may be extended to liking art that is incomprehensible (Joyce and Duchamp) and at the same time art that is too nose on your face (Satie). Such artists remain forever useful, useful I mean outside the museums, libraries, and conservatories in each moment of our daily lives. I happened one year to see a large exhibition of Dada in Düsseldorf. All of it had turned into art with the exception of Duchamp. The effect for me of Duchamp's work was to so change my way of seeing that I became in my way a duchamp unto my self. I could find as he did for himself the space and time of my own experience. The works signed by Duchamp are centrifugal. The world around becomes indistinguishable. In Düsseldorf it began with the light switches and electric outlets. One day after he had died Teeny Duchamp was taking me to see the *Etant Données* when it was still in New York before it went to Philadelphia. We were walking east along 10th Street. I said, needing some courage to do so: You know, Teeny, I don't understand Marcel's work. She replied: Neither do I. While he was alive I could have asked him questions, but I didn't. I preferred simply to be near him. I love him and for me more than any other artist of this century he is the one who changed my life, he and the younger ones who loved him too, Jasper Johns and Robert Rauschenberg. One day in the late '50s I saw him in Venice. I laughed and said: The year I was born you were doing what I'm doing now, chance operations. Duchamp smiled and said: I must have been fifty years ahead of my time.

For me Joyce is another story. When I was young I read *A Portrait of the Artist as a Young Man* and was not enthusiastic. At that time I loved the parts of *Finnegans Wake* that were published in *transition* and I often read them to entertain my friends. When the finished *Wake* was published I bought it but didn't think I had the time to read it. I was too busy writing music. Recently I have been punished. I have gone to Joyce as to a jail. I have made five writings through *Finnegans Wake*, and I've turned the second one into an hour-long radio play called *Roaratorio, An Irish Circus on Finnegans Wake*. As with Duchamp's work, so with Joyce's. And this goes for *Dubliners* and *Ulysses* too. I don't understand any of it. Nor do I understand the night sky with stars and moon in it. The fact we travel to the moon has given me no explanation of it. I would be delighted to retrace Bashō's steps in Japan, where as an old man he made a special tour on foot to enjoy particular views of the moon. When I was in Ireland for a month last summer ('79) with John and Monika Fullemann collecting sounds for *Roaratorio*, many Irishmen told me they couldn't understand *Finnegans Wake* and so didn't read it. I asked them if they understood their own dreams. They confessed they didn't. I have the feeling some of them may now be reading Joyce or at least dreaming they're reading Joyce. Adaline Glasheen says: "I hold to my old opinion. *Finnegans Wake* is a model of a mysterious universe made mysterious by Joyce for the purpose of striking with polished irony at the hot vanity of divine and human wishes." And she says: "Joyce himself told Arthur Power, 'What is clear and concise can't deal with reality, for to be real is to be surrounded by mystery.' Human kind, it is clear, can't stand much reality. We so fiercely hate and fear our cloud of unknowing that we can't believe sincere and unaffected, Joyce's love of the clear dark—it has got to be a paradox . . . an eccentricity of genius."

And Satie. I have analyzed his music and found it structured rhythmically. I have admired his choice of materials and his independent sense of form. His method it seems to me is a marriage of mode and the twelve tones. I think I know all that. But it does me no good. I have also studied wild mushrooms so that I won't kill myself when I eat what I find. I am always amazed how exciting it is in any season anywhere to see just any mushroom growing once again. The same is true each time I hear Satie well-played. I fall in love all over again.

I cheerfully set out to write the following text but for a week I could not put pen to paper. Then it occurred to me that all three, Joyce, Duchamp, Satie, since they are dead are ghosts and as such inhabit the same world we do. And I remembered a remark of Buckminster Fuller: that to give proper consideration to something one should begin not with one idea but with five. I decided to be cautious, to take five as a maximum, one as a minimum. Each of the three ghosts could be alone in which case he would read from his own writings. Or he could be together with another sentient being or beings, ghosts or living, or with a nonsentient being or beings. To outline the entire text then by means of chance operations was not difficult. There were twenty-six different possibilities: the three ghosts alone, each in combination with one to four different beings, the ghosts in pairs with one to three different beings, all three with one or two. I used the twenty-six letters of the alphabet and chance operations to locate facing pages of an unabridged dictionary upon which I found the nonsentient beings which are the stage properties of the various scenes (I through XXXVII) that follow. For the sentient beings, the other actors, I also used the alphabet, but only rarely as a means of finding a person I didn't know in an encyclopaedia. Mostly the other actors are people with whose work I've also become involved, sometimes as deeply as with Joyce, Duchamp, and Satie. Since many of the actors are ghosts, I have taken liberties with them, ascribing to them imaginary works they never made. I have also taken such liberties with those still alive. I hope no offense is received. It was not my intention to give any. The piece is not an alphabet: it is a fantasy. I did want to remove the punctuation, so to speak, from our experience of modernism, to illustrate it with something like its own excitement.

JAMES JOYCE, MARCEL DUCHAMP, ERIK SATIE: AN ALPHABET

I
what a Joy
to hAve
theM
on thE
Same stage same time

even though the subJect
Of
the plaY
is the Curtain
that sEparates them!

                    Justifying
              the constAnt
                          Moving up and down
              of thE curtain
              the ghoSts

                    Jump
         alternately fOrth and back and forth and forth
                    verY slowly
         in time with the Curtain's
                    phrasEology

              so that Just
                          As the curtain
         reaches the Midpoint
                          bEtween
         open and cloSed

                    Just
              at that mOment
         each ghost is halfwaY through a single jump
         (both their heads touChing
                          thE curtain)

              and Just
                          As the curtain reaches the top
                    Miraculously
              both of thEm
         complete their deScents   both are visible

                    and Just like magic
         as the curtain tOuches the floor
one of them disappears totallY from view leaving the other all alone
              in front of the Curtain
                    at that momEnt the telephone rings

an automated Judge
Answers it
and tells the audience whoM
thE call
iS for   it's always

for the ghost who has Just disappeared
whO cannot be reached
in this waY we know who
eaCh ghost is
but nEither ghost is distracted

from his Jumping
the older one is erik sAtie
he never stops sMiling
and thE younger one
iS joyce, thirty-nine

he Jumps
with his back tO the audience
for all we know he maY be quietly weeping
or silently laughing or both you just Can't
tEll

now and then niJinsky's ghost
Appears
bringing a telegraM
to joycE
from marShall mcluhan

Do you like that, *silenzioso*? Are you enjoying, this same little me, my life, my love? Why do you like my whisping? Is it not divinely deluscious? But in't it bafforyou? *Misi, misi!* Tell me till my thrillme comes! I will not break the seal. I am enjoying it still, I swear I am! Why do you prefer its in these dark nets, if why may ask, my sweetykins? Sh sh! Longears is flying. No, sweetissest, why would that ennoy me? But don't! You want to be slap well slapped for that. Your delighted lips, love, be careful! Mind my duvetyne dress above all! It's golded silvy, the newest sextones with princess effect.[1]

II   in the middle of one of his Jumps
                        sAtie grabbed hold of the curtain
          and instead of coMing down
                        ascEnded
                        hiS exit signals

                  the entrance of a Jeep
              which is truly an autOmobile   it needs no driver   it belongs
to no one   it is the invention of a 12-Year-old ghost
                        named duChamp
                        it is Expected

                        to iMprove the world
              it uses neither gAs
                        noR oil
              it runs on viChy
                        watEr
          the stage has become a bottLe of white wine

      and joyce no longer jumping is Drinking it.
                        oUt of the jeep
                        Come
                        cHildren going everywhere
              including A ghost four years old
                        naMed heidegger
          technology and Population

III   wE
                        heaR
                  over a radIo
          a conversation sticKing

                  to two wordS
                  fifty-five And
                        fifTy-four
                        It is
                  an argumEnt

                              bEtween houdini and satie
     about which one of them as a ghost is oldeR
                              houdIni
                    sees a cracK

                    in mathematicS
                              by meAns of which
                    aT
                              fIfty
          four and fivE

                              changE places
          satie is delighted and gRateful
                              now I see he says what people meant
                    thanK you

                    a flaSh of lightning
          is followed by A
                              loT of smoke
                              In which
          all the ghosts who arE

                    on thE stage
          easily disappeaR
                              houdIni and satie
          arm in arm walK on

     accompanied by a ceyloneSe ghost
                              a scholAr named coomaraswamy
          and a young acTor
                    and musIcian
          jonathan albErt

who isn't dEad at all
he's veRy much
alIve
he is speaKing

in hiS own
extrAordinary way
moving aT
wIll
from onE

rEgion of his mouth
to any of eight otheRs
followIng a notation
involving diacritical marKing

mine iS
A
movemenT system he says
I
makE

thE movement
and discoveR the sound.
meanwhIle
coomaraswamy is whispering a sansKrit text

IV   attracted by this duet Joyce returns
posthAste
to huM a program consisting of
onE
iriSh ballad

```
                two Japanese tunes
                      One
                melodY by satie
            and three lyriCal
                    suitEs


                     by fEldman feldman hasn't yet composed
                       noRmally
                         thIs would be impossible
          but for joyce it's no tricK at all


                    in fact it'S
                            As simple for him
                  as for him be biTten
                      by a radIsh
                    a scrap of papEr blows on stage


          following words're on it: Joyce
                           A
                         Music
                          hE
                          iS is music


              whether those are Just
                          lOose words in the air so to speak
                  or poetrY
                     by m. C. richards
                    no onE can be sure
```

Construction of a 4-dimensional eye From-: A circle (when seen by a 3-dimensional eye moving above and below until the visual ray falls in the plane which contains the circle) [a circle] undergoes many changes in shape conventionally determined by the laws of linear perspective. To-: (For the 3-dimensional eye a sphere remains always the same whatever the point of sight.) But a sphere (for the 4-dimensional perception moving in a 4-dimensional space until the 4-dimensional rays become visual rays for the ordinary 3-dimensional eye) [a sphere] undergoes many changes in shape, from 3-dimensional sphere gradually decreasing in volume without decreasing in radius, to simple plane circle. . . . Light and shade exist for 4-dimensional [objects] as for 3, 2, 1. Three-dimensional perspective starts in an initial *frontal plane without deformation*. Four-dimensional perspective will have a cube or 3-dimensional medium as a starting point which will not cause deformation i.e. in which the three-dimensional object is seen *circum-hyperhypo-embraced* (as if *grasped with the hand* and not seen with the *eyes*) -Just as a point intersects a curve and does not intersect a plane, so a curve of infinite length or *surface element* intersects a volume and does not intersect a 4-dimensional "solid." But either a plane or a surface intersects this 4-dimensional solid. -This 4-dimensional solid will be bounded by 3-dimensional volumes. *The shadow* cast by a 4-dimensional figure on our space is a *3-dimensional* shadow (see Jouffret "Géométrie à 4 dimensions" page 186, last three lines). *Three-dimensional sections of 4-dimensional figures by a space*: by analogy with the method by which architects depict the plan of each *story* of a house, a 4-dimensional figure can be represented (in each one of its stories) by 3-dimensional sections. These different *stories* will be bound to one another by the fourth dimension.[2]

V   thuMbing
     by meAns of a noninflammable match
      thRough an unabridged
       diCtionary
   duchamp noticEs three entries on facing pages
    two with iLlustrations

      reDheaded woodpecker
    wood titmoUse
    and woodCock
    this gives Him
     the ideA
       to Make readymobiles in unlimited editions
     and to Place the first one

     in a teMple
   just outside cAlcutta inhabited by the ghost
      of sRi ramakrishna that has been
 standing on one hand in eCstasy
      for ovEr ninety-three years
  duchamp picks up an inhaLator and breathes philadelphia

VI   buckMinster fuller
                        immediAtely
                        answeRs
                              Congratulating duchamp on all
              of his work past prEsent and future   he then goes on to say
                        my pLan for a regeneratively changing

              balance between unlimiteD
                              hUman needs
              and limited world resourCes is available
                  i am encouraged by tHe chincsc people
                        by the fAct
                  that one fourth of Mankind or one fifth if that's what it is
        is now relatively intelligent not just stuPidly political the way the rest

                  of the world is   i aM
                              Also
                        encouRaged by the youth
                  wherever they are   you Can
                              bE sure
              the young at some time wiLl spontaneously employ themselves

                  to change the worlD
                              they mUst however do it
                        quiCkly
                        wHile
                        necessAry below-earth energy sources
                        still reMain in sufficient quantity
                  to give needed initial Push

              to yet-to-be-invented world puMps
                              thAt
                  will ultimately opeRate by means of universe
                        eConomically
                        comprEhensively
                        and deLightfully

use insteaD of ownership
intUition instead of
Continuing
selfisHness
success for All
huManity instead of total oblivion
Possibility of realizing

good life for all Men depends
on reAlizing it
foR
eaCh
singlE man from a to z
Let us not forget the things

in the worlD
each one reqUires open-ended honor
Cease world pollution
initiate routes for speedy transport of eacH
refuse pArticle
to places in universe where what it cheMically is is in demand
see sPecialization as a drop in the bucket

-VII   the bucket is comprehensiveness   Joyce
is imAgining
a Mutton chop
and wondEring
where the next one'S to come from

you don't Just
find fOod
under Your feet
ghosts but nobody else Can
livE on thin air

64

VIII   Just a wee push   graffito graffiti
                                    to the Joy of us

                                 thrEe   three
                    jimmy and erik and teeny duShee

Furniture Music is fundamentally industrial. People have the habit—day
after day—of making music in situations where music has *nothing to do*.
Thus Waltzes, Fantasias from Operas, and other such things are played that
were written with another object in mind. What we want to do is to estab-
lish a music made to satisfy human needs the way the utilities do. Art is
extraneous to these needs. Furniture Music creates vibrations. That's its
single purpose. It plays the same role played by light, heat and all other
household conveniences. Furniture Music advantageously takes the place of
Marches, Polkas, Tangos, Gavottes, etc. Insist upon Furniture Music. Have
no meetings, no get-togethers, no social affairs of any kind without Furniture Music. Furniture Music for notaries, banks, etc. There's no difference
between one piece of Furniture Music and another (they all belong to the
same family). Don't get married without Furniture Music. Stay out of
houses that don't use Furniture Music. Anyone who hasn't heard Furniture
Music has no idea what true happiness is. If you go to sleep without first
listening to a piece of Furniture Music, you won't sleep well.[3] They can't
know anything about it. They don't read the newspaper I read every day.[4] If
you have three trumpets there isn't anything you can't do.[5] There are trees
on which you'll never see a bird; cedars, for instance. These trees are so dark
that birds get bored on them, and avoid them. Poplars are no longer visited.
Getting to them is dangerous: they're much too high.[6] Like money, the
piano's only pleasing to the person who has his hands on it.[7] The sea is full
of water. Why we'll never know.[8]

IX   duchaMp
                                    monDrian

                         and Joyce go into the mind of krishna
                      lao-tse Jogs

                    early in the Morning on the great wall of china
                       wilD duck

satiE visits
conlon nancaRrow
In mexico city
he is Knocked out

by nancarrow'S music
for two plAyer pianos
when he comes To
he announces the decIsion
nExt

timE he listens
to do so flat on the flooR
not on hIs stomach
but on his bacK

hiS decision
puts ideAs
in The
pIano
mEchanisms

nancarrow turns thEm on
satie lies on the flooR
the pIanos move toward him
but in the nicK of time they thematically

pull themSelves up
so there's sufficient spAce
for Them
to roll over hIm without hurting him
in thE

lEast   satie is touched
but not physically   i am veRy
pIanistic he says
but i have never Known

                    Such
               good behAvior
                    on The part
               of musIcal
               instrumEnts

                    i will writE about it
               in the newspapeRs
                    the telephone rIngs
          it is a mr. robert m. quacKen-

                    buSh, 460 e. 79th street
               n. y. c. u. s. A.   the pianos speak up
                         whaT does he want?   we want to know
               what he wants   nothIng
                    he has thE wrong—

                    satiE says goodbye
               to nancaRrow: au rentendre
          you've shown me somethIng new   i am bowled over
               and grateful   you maKe me want to write music again

XI   Joyce
                    is At work
               in a roMan bank
                    mErce cunningham
                    comeS in to cash a traveler's check

                    Just sign
               giambattista vicO's name
                    instead of Your own
               and i'll give you Control
                    of a rEvolving fund

that will keep your company Jumping
in An honorable way
froM now until dublinsday
cunningham asks how to spEll it
joyce replieS

don't spell it at all Just write it
dOwn
as though You
were danCing.
your drEams

havE all been
tRue.
XII   ghosts shouldn't stay In houses merely frightening
single families   they should walK out into the world

and haunt everyone continuouSly
until the revolutions ghosts begAn
while They were
lIving
arE completed

china was Just
A beginning
as far as i aM
concErned   i want to lengthen
the long retreat So it extends through the rest

of the world   Jesus was right
Or
don't You think so?
i am only a Child
and so i can lEad you

                    mao tsE-tung has spoken
                       thoReau veblen joyce
                    and satIe
                    continue walKing and running

            in different orbitS
                              Around him playing the game called
                       ludwig That's sun surrounded by planets
    and planets surrounded by moons   It's midnight
                    at waldEn pond

                          Just then
                          A
                          luMinous glass
                          suddEnly
                          appearS poised in space

        toward it 4-year-old mao directs a Jet
                                    Of destructive thin air
                    which is instantaneouslY diverted by thoreau who explains
                          i proteCt
                          my invEntion:

                          a winE glass
                          whateveR
                          you put In it   no matter what
                    anything you liKe   even dirt will do

            everything becomeS wine
                       there's A
                          swiTch
                       for changIng colors
                       and anothEr for changing its size

                                                                    69

                              to that of a Jigger
                                    or enlArging it
                        to that of a Mug
                              its namE
                                    changeS according to what you want in it

              vodka or stout or whatever Just
                                    One glass exists   it has
        a krishna feature so it can be used bY any number of people at the same time
              no matter where they are   it's Communist
                        says mao tsE-tung

                              it's tEchnical says veblen
                              it's iResh says joyce
                        c'est admIrable says satie
        all ghosts at once: how did you thinK of it?

                                    anSwer: i don't know
              i never drink   i wAs
                              jusT
                              takIng
                        anothEr step in the direction

                              of siMplicity
        XIII   duchAmp
              has on a caRpenter's outfit
                        he Clips
                              to Each pocket
                        a smaLl

                                    carD 1½ inches wide and 2 inches high
        each card has a different pictUre on it by utrillo, utamaro,
                        or uCello
                              tHus
                        he tAkes on the character
                        of a Museum
              with no need for sPecial

                    proMotion
                    progrAms
            because all the aRt it owns
                    Can
                       bE seen without going inside
   or buying a ticket without any troubLe at all

               if one of the carDs is stolen
                    or boUght
                    he replaCes it
                    witH
                          Another which is not
               exactly the saMe
               that keeps the Public

                  on the Move never sure
                       whAt's being shown
         duchamp counts the caRds
                    periodiCally
                          and Each time he reaches thirty-three
               he makes a sLight

                    aDdition
            to the thirty-foUrth which he finds amusing
               and the Critics find upsetting
                    tHey
                       Are continually
            changing their Minds
   because their minds always sPring back to the way they were

            in the first place alMost
                    immediAtely
               duchamp caRries a whisk broom
               and if a Critic
                    drops somEthing he whisks it up
            and puts it in a vaLise

markeD
              Unsigned memorabilia
    he is thinking of investing in a Cuisinart
              to cHop up this collection
              to mAke it into a large single work untitled
    in advance later to be known as *infraMation*
              sPatial

XIV   the scene changes   duchaMp
                    hAs taken off
                the caRpenter's outfit
            but the Card
            musEum
                    foLlows him anyway

            each carD faces
                    oUtward from him
        has no visible Connection
            to Him
            it's quite mArvelous
            he's a Museum
            without Pockets

        and he has a suMmer
            plAce
        on the costa bRava   that's where hc is now
            he Can
            bE
    outdoors beside an oLive tree

                    Drinking spring water
            or inside oUt of the sun
        eating some peas or *Céleri rémoulade*
                    He limits himself
                to A teaspoonful whether it's solid
        or liquid   it occurs to hiM that utamaro has no first name
    in the dictionary   taking maurice and Paolo

                as alphabetical liMits
                        And
            thinking of bRown he is on the point
                of Choosing n.o.
                whEn
                    the teLephone rings   it's philip glass

            this gives him the iDea of an indeterminate first name
                    having Unlimited repetitions of letters
    n.n. oooooouooo for instanCe
                        pHilip
                    didn't sAy a word except hello
                        Marcel thanks him
                        Playfully

    XV   bob rauschenberg coMes in
                it must be your deAthday
                        i've bRought you a present
                it's an ameriCan
                        jEt
                with a portabLe airport

                part of the lanDing gear
            are these rolled-Up runways
                        that Can be put in your pocket
                        and tHen when you need them
                        you tAke
                            theM out
                        and droP both through a slot

                in the Men's room
                            And then they automatically expand
                    to the pRoper length in the proper position
    just as the plane is touChing
                        thE ground
                        the pLane itself is no larger than

                a vitamin pill   what Do
                        yoU think of it?
          it's obviously an exCellent device says marcel
                but i tHink
                        thAt you should keep it
                where it caMe from
          my travels are telePathic

                        pure and siMple
                                All i have to do is think
                        of anotheR
                                City
                        and thEn i'm there
                i don't need to fLy

                        what i Do is
                remain as thoUghtless
                        as i Can
                                otHerwise
                                i'm constAntly traveling   never at rest
          just yesterday i was in Madagascar
          and this morning i was in Paris

                        when i just Mention
                                these plAces to you
          i can feel myself beginning to be transpoRted
                                i have to quiCkly think
                                of thE
                                        pLace where i am

                        in orDer
                to continUe
                        our Conversation
                being a gHost
                        hAs
                its probleMs
          would you like to Play chess?

                    i know the Moves
                  but thAt's about all
          come sometime to floRida
                    and teaCh
                       mE
                     i wiLl

The parasols thus *straighten out* the spangles which, on leaving the tubes, were free and wished to rise. They *straighten them out* like a sheet of paper rolled up too much which one unrolls several times in the opposite direction. *to the point that:* necessarily there is a change of condition in the spangles. They can no longer *retain their individuality* and they all *join* together after B. *The illuminating gas* (II). *After B. —change in the condition of the spangles.—* From their *dizziness* (provisional), from their *loss* of awareness of position, *obtained* by successive passing through the sieves and imperceptible change of direction of these sieves (change of direction of which the terminations are A and B), the spangles (dissolve); the spangles splash themselves each to itself, i.e. change (little by little through the last sieves) their condition *from: spangles lighter than air, of a certain length, of elemental* thickness with a determination to rise, *into*: a liquid elemental scattering, seeking no direction, a *scattered suspension* on their way out at B, Vapor of inertia, snow, but keeping its liquid *character* through instinct for cohesion (the only manifestation of the *individuality* (so reduced!!) of the illuminating gas in its habitual games with conventional surroundings. What a drip! Ventilator-*Churn.* (perhaps give it a butterfly form[9]

XVI   satiE
                  is giving a conceRt
                       of hIs
                   recent worK

                      kineSthetic music of contingency
              it is performed by Animals
                  the soloisTs are
          an octopus and a fIsh hawk
                  all sEctions

of thE
oRchestra
are fIlled with butterflies of various sizes
except for an enormous Koto

which iS
the stAge
iTself
the anImals
and insEcts

arE themselves
the instRuments
each has a broadcastIng system and each member of the audience
has his own receiver and loudspeaKing

headSet
the flights of the musiciAns
and The promenade of the octopus
are perfectly beautIful
to hEar

and to sEe
the audience is as quiet as a mouse   eveRy now and then
one of the musIcians
happens to play the Koto   sometimes producing a melody

sometimes Just
-XVII   A single tone   joyce no sooner sent out
the invitations to his party than alMost
Everyone arrived
homer waS the first   he was singing a revision

of his *iliad*   for open house the house is Just right
eccles street is actually Open   nothing but a vacant lot with brick
façade between it and the street   joseph beuYs
who has Caught
two phEasants   one silver one gold

is about to explain Joyce's
wAke
to theM
Even though
joyce of courSe is there and they are alive

he begins with his Jaw
nOt speaking
but moving it sidewaYs
the birds watCh him
attEntively

then he Jigs
A jog
the pheasants respond by Marching
in quickstEp
So erratically the guests are obliged

to levitate   he rips his Jacket
tO pieces
this makes the pheasants so happY
they Can't
contain thEmselves

they Jump on his shoulders
And then take off
in the direction of the Moon
lEaving
two featherS behind

Just
befOre
theY disappear
beuys touChing
his forEhead with both feathers

                    thinks Jungle
                     this Acts
                    like Magic
                      thE
                    pheaSants reappear

                     Just
                 as thOugh they'd never left
      in exchange for the feathers beuYs gives the birds
                    felt eleCtric
                        nEsts that can be plugged in anywhere

The more you're with musicians, the crazier you get.[10] On the hour, a servant takes my temperature and gives me back another.[11] I'd never dare at-
tack anyone . . . anyone who doesn't think the way I do. Thought is the
property of the person who has it. No one else has the right to even touch
it.[12] You want to know how to become a musician? It's very simple. You get
a teacher, a music teacher, and you go with him as far as possible. Choose
him carefully . . . You'll have to buy a metronome. Make sure it isn't too
ripe, and above all it should have some flesh on it and a little fat. Make sure
it works well. Because there are some metronomes that work the wrong
way. Just like idiots. You'll even come across some that don't work at all.
These are not good metronomes. Afterwards, I'd advise you to buy something to put your music in, a brief case. They come at all prices. *The problem you'll have is deciding which one you want.* A student should have lots
of patience, great patience, the patience of a horse, huge patience. Because
it's very beneficial for a student to get used to putting up with his teacher.
Just think: a teacher! He'll ask questions he knows and that you, you don't
know. He takes unfair advantage, obviously. But you have the right to remain silent. *It's even the best policy.* Don't take it out on your instrument.
Instruments often submit to very bad treatment. *People beat them.* I've
known children who took pleasure in stepping on the feet of their piano.
Others don't put their violins back in their cases. And then, poor thing, it
gets a chill and catches cold. *That's not nice.* Not at all. And some pour
snuff into their trombones. This is very unpleasant *for the instrument.* And
when they blow on it they project those irritating particles into the faces of
people around them, and then everyone sneezes and coughs, sometimes for
over half an hour. Ugh! The consequences are serious. And afterwards the
instrument works poorly and has to be fixed. You do your exercises in the
morning, after breakfast. You should be very clean, and you should have

blown your nose. You shouldn't start working with your fingers covered with jam. The hours and the days you take lessons have to be scheduled with the consent of both the pupil and the teacher. It would be very inconvenient if the pupil took his lesson at his hour on his day while the teacher gave it at another hour on another day. That goes on all the time in schools. There are some students who never lay eyes on their teachers. Curious application of an educational system. Don't follow that plan. Because, out of necessity, there has to be some agreement. The pupil, and the teacher, were put on this earth to meet one another. At least from time to time. Otherwise, where would we get? That's right, where would we? I'll tell you. We'd get *nowhere*. Realize that work is freedom. Freedom that is for everybody else. While you work, you don't bother anybody. Never forget it. You understand? Sit down. I'm obliged to finish this talk an hour ahead of time. Soon it will be six. I have to have something to eat. Then I want to take a walk in order to get an appetite. Children, please be good.[13]

XVIII   duchaMp
                            And satie
                        aRe alone   i'm glad to be with you
                    we Can look
                        at thE sceneries or have a conversation
            is there anything you Like to say?

                    i've just talkeD my head off
                        my laUgh
                what is that? an inCandescent lamp?
            i've never seen sucH
                            A big one! what's it doing here
            backstage?   it Magrittes me think
                it's using uP

                    all thE
                        eneRgy
                    there Is
                        looK!   i'm right!

the other lightS
                    Are
                noT
                workIng
                any longEr!

XIX   satiE
                    goes in seaRch
                        of sunlIght   he comes across haydn
            bill anastasi is looKing at haydn through a lorgnette

                        but Seems
                    to be tAking
                    a phoTograph
                        bIll
                        Explains

                that thE
                    loRgnette
            connected to an old televIsion set acts as a secondary camera
                enabling him to taKe the picture

                    of a ghoSt
                    of A
                    ghosT
                    provIding
                        Everything

                    anD everyone
                before dUring and after the photograph's taken
                are in exaCtly
                    the rigHt positions
XX   sAtie says
                i have soMe music
                that is to be Played

                    Silently
        i wrote it with An invisible ink and luckily
        i gave the manuscripT to duchamp
              one of these nIghts i'll ask him
                    for a xErox of it

   XXI   joycE joins satie
              they sit about thRee feet apart
                          and facIng one another
                    the clocK

                          Strikes
                          And
                    the seaTed
                          beIng
                    in thE

                          spacE between them   half dead and half alive
        ibsen on one side and isou on the otheR
                                begIns to revolve on a smoothly operating
              table so that after satie has talKed to

                          ibSen
                          And isou
                          To joyce
                          It is isou
                    who makEs

                          a rEply to satie
   and satie who makes one to isou   whoeveR—and
                                thIs also applies to ibsen and joyce—
                    whoever is talKing

                          iS interrupting the other
              the following is A short sample
                          of whaT
                          was saId:
                          "E

                              my bEd
                           is Round
                           Ic
                           K"

XXII   Joyce
              is sitting in the entrAnce hall
                 of an ancient roMan
                         housE watching the rain come in
                  what iS that called   that basin

              in which a pool is Just beginning
                         tO form?
                    replY: the impluvium below,
                    the Compluvium
                    abovE   the compluvium is the open space

                 in the roof   Joyce's mind
                         wAnders
                    froM
                    rain to rivEr to ocean
                           he iS doing the australian crawl

          in south america where Juruá
                              jOins amazon
          now he's on his back on lake nYasa
                    in afriCa
                           hE rides

          the norwegian falls of skykJefos
                              And then goes the length
                    of the Mississippi
                         twicE   once in a boat
          and once walking on the water itSelf

he goes to the top of kanchenJunga
                  frOm which he sees
     all the himalaYan rivers
     taking different direCtions
                  to form thE mouths of the ganges

     he says i loved the skykJefos so much i wonder
          if i took the form of A
                    salMon
                    whEther
               i could riSe from its foot to its head

                    Just
               the thOught's
     what's necessarY   from norway
          he goes to California
                    and doEs the same thing up yosemite

not troubling to salmonize himself he Just goes
                    As he is
               he swiMs
               for a yEar
          in all partS of ocean

               from Japan
                    thrOugh indian and atlantic
               to Yarmouth
          through arCtic and pacific
               to nEw zealand

               he is Joined
               by whAles
          one of whoM swallows him
                    washEd up whight and deliveried rhight
          loud laudS to his luckhump

and bEjetties on jonahs![14]

XXIII
satie is veRy busy
ebenezer prout Is
giving him a quicK

leSson
in hArmony melody
rhyThm
counterpoInt
and orchEstration

in half an hour in athEns he has an appointment
with a second-centuRy poet
whose name Is oppian
oppian's well Known

for hiS three long poems
one on fishing And
anoTher
on huntIng
and thE third on birdcatching

the sEcond
and thiRd are now thought
to have been wrItten by another poet of the same name
while prout corrects errors satic quicKly

lookS in his book
And sees
he's To have lunch
wIth
dovE bradshaw

what a dElight!   he says
i like heR
and her drawIngs very much   they are both so healthy
i must asK her

                    what exerciSes she gives her pencils
          not possible! cocktAils
                    wiTh
               mrs. natIon!
                    carriE nation!

               i can't bElieve it!
                    pRout
                         gIves him
               a tasK:

               fourthS
                    And
               fifThs
                         In diagonal motion
          i'll do that in fivE

                    minutEs says satie
          on my way to gReece
          the telephone rIngs
          he answers it   thanK heaven!

                    She isn't free!
               his secretAry hands him a new supply
          of music paper That came
                    wIth
               his nExt compositions

               in pEncil
                    alReady
               on It
          all he has to do is inK them in

     greece   the voice of oppian: "there'S no music i love
                              more thAn yours   would you consider
                    playing my furniTure
                         or teachIng it to play you?
                    i can't tEll you how comfortable that'd make me

All through my youth people said, "You'll see when you're fifty." I'm fifty. I see nothing.[15] You want to know whether I'm French? Of course I am. Why would you want a man of my age not to be French? You surprise me.[16] Personally, I am neither good nor bad. I oscillate, if I may say so. Also, I've never really done anyone any harm—nor any good, to boot.[17] A child has natural wisdom: he knows everything. Experience is one of the forms of paralysis.[18] An artist is certainly worthy of respect, but a listener is even more so. Why is it easier to bore people than it is to entertain them?[19]

XXIV and how is Joyce
                          Affected by charcoal?
                 it fills hiM with admiration
               for it is largEly pure
                          iS carbon

                 is ancient Jewel, hardest substance
                 diamOnd
                          sYmbol as an element
                 is C
                 is widEly distributed

                          Joined with other sources
          energizes some of the stArs
                 its coMpounds
                 in numbEr exceed
                          thoSe of all other elements combined

                 is not Just fuel
                          thOugh as such
                          Yields a larger amount of heat
          in proportion to its volume than Can
                          bE obtained from a corresponding

       quantity of wood   makes no smoke   Just
                          mAkes fire   finely divided is efficient
       to filter adsorption of gases'n'solids froM solution
                          is usEd in the purification of water and air
                          in gaS masks and the refining of sugar

is made to Jump
        tO greater heights of adsorptiveness
        bY means
of speCial
        hEating or chemical processes

such forced Jump's
        Activated charcoal
aniMal black's
    its namE
    when it'S obtained not from wood but from bones

        Judged
        nOt father but mother of coal
when fine it took the forms of laYers between beds
    of bituminous Coal
        pEncil or crayon

    or Just
        A piece of paper
artist has used to Mark upon
        is bElieved
        to exiSt free in nature in a form that's white

that has not yet been found spirit has adJusted us
        tO
    its eventual discoverY
        Charcoal writing
        whitE'r'black upon white'r'black

    conJecture:
    the cAtholic
        Mass
    is a charcoal ovEn: the making of bread
    the body of chriSt

We must bring about a music which is like furniture, a music, that is, which will be part of the noises of the environment, will take them into considera-tion. I think of it as melodious, softening the noises of the knives and forks, not dominating them, not imposing itself. It would fill up those heavy si-lences that sometimes fall between friends dining together. It would spare them the trouble of paying attention to their own banal remarks. And at the same time it would neutralize the street noises which so indiscretely enter into the play of conversation. To make such music would be to respond to a need.[20] Everyone'll tell you that I'm not a musician. That's right. From the beginning of my career, I classed myself among phonometrographers. My works are pure phonometry. No musical idea presided at the creation of my works. Scientific thought was in charge. I take more pleasure in measuring a sound than I do in hearing one. If I have a phonometer in my hand, I work with joy and confidence. What haven't I weighed or measured? All of Bee-thoven, all of Verdi, etc. It's very strange. The first time I used a phonoscope, I examined a B flat of average size. Never I assure you have I ever seen anything more disgusting. I called my servant and had him look at it. On a phonoscale, an ordinary F sharp, run of the mill, came to 93 kilograms. It came out of a very fat tenor whose weight I also took. Do you know any-thing about cleaning sounds? It's a very dirty business. Working in a cotton mill is cleaner. To know how to classify sounds is very painstaking and you have to have good eyes. As for sonorous explosions, often so disagreeable, cotton in your ears attenuates them and makes them endurable. This is pyrophony. I think I can say that phonology is superior to music. It has more variety. It is more profitable. I owe my fortune to it. In any case, with a motodynamophone, a phonometricist with very little experience can easily notate more sounds than the most experienced musician given the same amount of time and effort. It is because of that that I've been able to get so much written. The future therefore is in the field of philophony.[21]

XXV   vase   Joyce is writing
                                   A letter to nora—he is
     in the next to last paragraph   his Mind and body
                                   thEir feet in poetry
                           from her aS flower in hedges

          excited move to her as obJect
                        hOg she is sow
                  of his everY
                      filthy Craving
                  no inch of hEr body   no odour sight sound nor act of it

```
                but's irresistible   Joy
                      of An
                orgasM
                  swEetheart
                  anSwer me


XXVI                          Joyce
                  mAking use of thirteen letters
        written to hiM
                  by Ezra pound
                  writeS the following mesostics on his own name


    can't make out whether Jean
                      de gOurmont wants to translate
                  anY
                handsChrift
                  morE illegible


                  than Jim
                  ms. Arrived
            this a.M.
        wish you Every
                      poSsible success


                  cher J.
            i dunnO
            no lawYer
      in return for whiCh
                      rEcd. several


              dear Jim:
                  Answered
                  Miss-
                firE
          that omitS the essential
```

                    J.: first number
                Of
                mY
        new periodiCal
                dEsigned

                    Juvenile indiscretions
                mAy now
        cash in on 'eM
                    thE noble gerhardt
                    iS struggling both with

                    J-J-J-Jayzus
                ribbOn iz pale
                    You better have
                the Carbon
                thE

                    Joyce
                wAnts
                xMas
                likE what gabriel
                Said to

                    Jean
                de gOurmont
                anY
            handsChrift
        is morE

            dear Jim
                    Arrived
        this a.M.
                    Every
                poSsible

                              J.
                         dunnO no
                         lawYer
                         whiCh
                           rEcd. several

XXVII   duchaMp
                               sAtie
                         leonaRdo
                         da vinCi
                         and thE poet
                                   Louis zukofsky are writing a japanese poem

    they have themselves photographeD
                              with fUjiyama   the average person would think
                         it was just a piCture
                         of tHe
                         mountAin
                    because none of theM   none of the ghosts   can be seen
                    at all   however the Photograph

                              is a linE in the poem which goes on as follows:
                    angels and bastaRds
             how do you catch such a bIrd?
                    poor songster weaK

                    gold, white, plaSter, indigo
                         without primAry shadow
                         carefully scoTch tapes
                    the germans stIll advancing
                         at thE opera

                              soMe of them go round the fields
                         relAted as equated
                         by eRos' matrix
             transfer from one like objeCt
                    who's in lovE with me
                              of Labor light lights in air

transposeD by the perspective

to raise dUst on dust—

straight line, Curve, etc.

splasHes which should be

spiders love music just As

encounter at the bottoM

all gay where how sPill lay who

a straight horizontal thrEad

Rope, mercury, cloth

of what Is in what is not

gold or silver or the liKe

done in the Semi

3rd of the width of the leAf

and ouT of respect

columns on the walls In front

of thE count of urbino[22]

Dictionary—with films, taken close up, of parts of very large objects, obtain photographic records which no longer look like photographs of something. With these semi-microscopics constitute a dictionary of which each film would be the representation of a group of words in a sentence or separated so that this film would assume a new significance or rather that the concentration on this film of the sentences or words chosen would give a form of meaning to this film and that, once learned, this relation between film and meaning translated into words would be "striking" and would serve as a basis for a kind of writing which no longer has an alphabet or words but signs (films) already freed from the "baby talk" of all ordinary languages.— Find a means of filing all these films in such order that one could refer to them as in a dictionary. "Theory" 10 words found by opening the dictionary at random by A   10 words found by opening the dictionary at random by B[23]

XXVIII   the ghost of brighaM young
                    is speAking   i am happy to announce
           that puRsuant
        to our many Conversations
      duchamp has accEpted an anonymous mormon commission
      to make another Large work

     it will have many briDes and fewer bachelors
       it will be a compUterized
         series of glass Cubes
                tHere will be movement
           of gAses lights and liquids
           froM one cube to another
           a sPecial

     architectural attachMent
          is being mAde to house it
   so that it can go on touR
  it will be simple to detaCh it
         from onE building
            and cLip it on to the next

  it will have a map of the worlD connected to it
          like those sUbway maps in paris that light up
       you piCk out
         tHe city it's to go to
           And when the lights go on
  after a short delay which perMits the correction
           of Possible errors and pinpointing

of precise destination the building Moves
          without Any passage of time at all
       to the place wheRe it's supposed to go
       its basiC
         homE of course
         wiLl be

                    philaDelphia
                    bUt
            for speCial occasions once a year at least
it will be sHown
        in sAlt lake city
        the nuMber of brides
        is still uP in the air but several things

are certain   there will be More brides
                thAn
                bacheloRs
                    eaCh
                    bridE
                    wiLl

            be four-Dimensional
        and have a plUrality
                of aCcelerations
    infra connections with eacH of the cubes
            i suggested one bAchelor instead of several
the single bachelor could be the prograM itself in the form of
    a jack-in-the-box   duchamP

                seeMs to like
            the ideA
        too many bacheloRs he says
    might bring about impraCtical conjugations
                    wE must avoid excessive
        technicaLity

XXIX   mozart satiE
            and schoenbeRg
                    are gIving three concerts at once
    in the same place   capers   Kangaroo

XXX

satiE
is having tRouble
wIth his shoelaces
they Keep coming untied

he telephoneS louise nevelson
louise he sAys i'm afraid
They
wIll
loosEn

my Sense
of hArmony
i have made an appoinTment
wIth
sigmund frEud to have them analyzed

XXXI

Joyce
And
duchaMp
arE looking
at a twelve-Sided astrological television set

if your seat Jibes
with yOur sign
the commercials're not visible to You
instead you automatiCally
gEt your horoscope

Morris
grAves
appeaRs by satellite
from Calcutta
and dakhinEswar
he enters a tempLe of kali

he places before the image of the goDdess
an offering of frUit
it is reCeived
for He
leAves
returns to his rooM in the hotel in calcutta
and Paints a picture

duchamp and Joyce enjoy seeing
(it is A zodiac
giving new forMs
to thE
Signs)

they speak as one person   Just fact
fOrm's taken for granted
makes it necessarY
to find way baCk
to how it was bEfore

forMs
cAme
into being   Rules are for games
but Chaos
is lifE
breaking Laws is what poetry is

language in particular must be changeD
even what yoU eat
Can't be mere following
of conventions eitHer
stArt
froM breath   from zero
Possibility of no-mind

XXXII   satiE is conducting
                          his wateR
                                    musIc in fire movements   the first is called
            pine cones   it is damp and smoKy

XXXIII   Joyce
                                  imAgines
                        nora's in the rooM
                            no nEed for perfume
                        and muSic   she is his own

XXXIV   his maJesty
                                  hAs fallen to pieces
                      joyce is picking theM up
                            parnEll
                            iS

                                  Just
                      six letters Of the alphabet
                that go together in different waYs
                            not Changing
                            thEir sequence, not making anagrams

            six fragments of his irish maJesty
                                  cAnnot be found in *finnegans wake*
      and strangely enough arne is one of theM
                            Even though
                      arne compoSed *rule britannia*

            other fragments you'd Just
                            nOt expect (r.n. for instance) are there
                      in fact onlY between a tenth and a third
                            aCcording to how you count
                      of uncrownEd king's missing

I no longer have any notion of time or space; sometimes it even happens that I don't know what I'm saying.[24] Erik Satie, Dear Sir, Eight years ago I was suffering from a polyp in my nose complicated by liver trouble and rheumatism. On hearing your *Ogives*, I noticed an improvement in my health; four or five applications of your *Third Gymnopédie* cured me completely. I authorize you, Mr. Erik Satie, to make any use you wish of this testimonial.[25] Before writing one of my works, I walk around it several times, and I get myself to go with me.[26]

XXXV   Just
                                        A coincidence
                    that their initials are both Minimally
                                        lEttered
                                    the Same letter

                                        a J
                                        a) Of
                            an inventorY
                            of what in Common
                                    thEy have

                                    Joyce
                                    And johns
                        b and c) Mind spirit body
                                at homE
                                in homeS

                                    not Just
                                    One
                                everYone
                                    Colors
                                    idEas etc.   complexity   impartiality

            d) elegance in the enJoyment
                                    And expression of vulgarity
                                exaMination
                            of thE commonplace
                arrangementS for its return to mystery

```
        e) subJect's
    neither whOle nor part
    possibilitY of both
        Continuing
        bEcoming
```

night by silentsailing night while infantina Isobel (who will be blushing all
day to be, when she growed up one Sunday, Saint Holy and Saint Ivory, when
she took the veil, the beautiful presentation nun, so barely twenty, in her
pure coif, sister Isobel, and next Sunday, Mistlemas, when she looked a
peach, the beautiful Samaritan, still as beautiful and still in her teens, nurse
Saintette Isabelle, with stiffstarched cuffs but on Holiday, Christmas, Easter
mornings when she wore a wreath, the wonderful widow of eighteen
springs, Madame Isa Veuve La Belle, so sad but lucksome in her boyblue's
long black with orange blossoming weeper's veil) for she was the only girl
they loved, as she is the queenly pearl you prize, because of the way the
night that first we met she is bound to be, methinks, and not in vain, the
darling of my heart, sleeping in her april cot, within her singachamer, with
her greengageflavoured candywhistle dùetted to the crazyquilt, Isobel, she
is so pretty, truth to tell, wildwood's eyes and primarose hair, quietly, all the
woods so wild, in mauves of moss and daphnedews, how all so still she lay,
neath of the whitethorn, child of tree, like some losthappy leaf, like blowing
flower stilled, as fain would she anon, for soon again 'twill be, win me, woo
me, wed me, ah weary me! deeply, now evencalm lay sleeping; nowth upon
nacht, while in his tumbril Wachtman Havelook seequearscenes, from yon-
sides of the choppy, punkt by his curserbog, went long the grassgross bump-
instrass that henders the pubbel to pass, stowing his bottle in a hole for at
whet his whuskle to stretch ecrooksman, sequestering for lovers' lost prop-
ertied offices the leavethings from allpurgers' night, og gneiss ogas gnasty,
kikkers, brillers, knappers and bands, handsboon and strumpers, sminky-
sticks and eddiketsflaskers;[27]

XXXVI   suzuki, kwang-tse and Joyce
                give us A word
              instead of reMaining
                 silEnt
                      aS you've remained now for three days

subJect's reality
what wOuld
            You say?   this table's real?   yes
            Can you
            tEll us what way?

            Just to rolywholyover
      yes in every wAy
and yesterday when that Man
            spokE
            you Said what he said was good

      you didn't obJect
            were yOu
            butterflY?
      or were you beComing a man?
                  in zEn you said most important thing is life

            and Just
            todAy
      when this other Man
            spokE
            you alSo said what he said was good

   again you didn't obJect
            (nOr did he:
            onlY true answer serves
      to set all well afloat) but how Can you?
                  in zEn you said most important thing is death

            it is Just
            thAt in zen
      there is not Much
            diffErence between the two
                  Sutra (the sanskrit, a thread, a string)

XXXVII
                           duchaMp telephones
                            from kAnsas
      it's like nothing on eaRth   i feel as i did
                  before beComing a ghost
                      i havE no regrets
                     i weLcome whatever happens next

NOTES

1. James Joyce. *Finnegans Wake* (New York: Viking Press, edition embodying all author's corrections), pp. 147–148.

2. Marcel Duchamp. *Salt Seller: The Writings of Marcel Duchamp*, edited by Michel Sanouillet and Elmer Peterson (New York: Oxford University Press, 1973), pp. 88–89.

3. Erik Satie. *Ecrits*, réunis, établis et annotés par Ornella Volta (Paris: Editions Champ Libre, 1977), p. 190. (Translation by John Cage.)

4. Satie, p. 160.	10. Satie, p. 153.	15. Satie, p. 45.
5. Satie, p. 159.	11. Satie, p. 23.	16. Satie, p. 28.
6. Satie, p. 153.	12. Satie, p. 91.	17. Satie, p. 26.
7. Satie, p. 154.	13. Satie, pp. 82–85.	18. Satie, p. 173.
8. Satie, p. 162.	14. Joyce, p. 358.	19. Satie, p. 165.
9. Duchamp, p. 50.		

20. John Cage. *Silence* (Middletown, CT: Wesleyan University Press, 1961), p. 76.

21. Satie, p. 19.

22. A mix of lines from Louis Zukofsky, *"A"* (Berkeley: University of California Press, 1978); *The Notebooks of Leonardo da Vinci*, compiled and edited from the original manuscripts by Jean Paul Richter (New York: Dover Publications, 1970); Duchamp; and Satie.

23. Duchamp, p. 78.	25. Satie, p. 113.	27. Joyce, p. 556.
24. Satie, p. 155.	26. Satie, p. 143.	

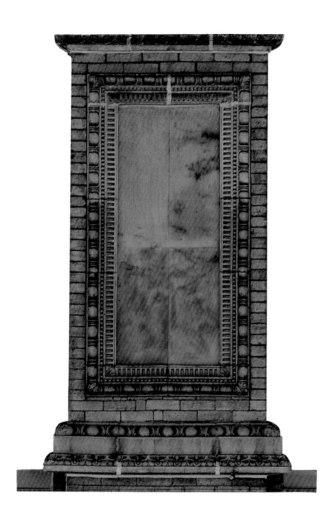

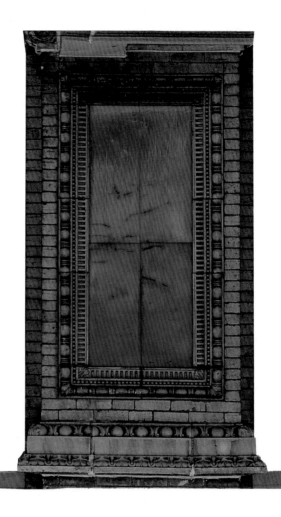

In 1970 *Song* was written as a text for *Solo for Voice 35* in the *Song Books*. The melodic line was the second movement of *Cheap Imitation*, which keeps the phraseology of Erik Satie's *Socrate* but varies the melody. *Song*, published as a poem in *M*, was derived by means of *I Ching* chance operations from the *Journal* of Henry David Thoreau, each line chosen from a particular part of a particular page of one of its fourteen volumes.

When I first saw Susan Barron's photographs of fields, weeds, woods, lakes, I was delighted by them and offered to write a text to accompany them in a limited edition. I had in mind to write mesostics on the names of the seasons, spring, summer, autumn, and winter. I got nowhere with this project until I sat down one day in The Hague, looked out the window and wrote mesostics which were "photographs" of what was at that moment happening. This seemed interesting to attempt but not appropriate for photographs of nature (I was in a theater looking out on a playground with a city street beyond). Several months later it occurred to me to go again through the process that had produced *Song* (Satie's title for the second movement of the *Socrate* is *On the Banks of the Ilissus*) and thus to write *Another Song* for Susan Barron.

ANOTHER SONG

Rabbits, musquash
snipe, but hear none
fog for four days
countless swallows.

Now, in shallow places near the bends
distinguished by its blueness
the air is full of falling leaves
turning round and round and scratching with its claws. A shower
a basketful of Irish moss.

Etc.
it looks as if
the most rugged walking is on the steep westerly slope. We had a grand view.

As he looks back
I return, the sun is rising and the
walls were one reflector with countless facets.

They say that the Indians
used to find them in the brooks.

Two ducks sailing, partly white
New Testament.

Down to its grave
and does not die
put it on
and buckle it
tighter.

Pause of the slow-blooded creature
the rocks.

The hills eight or ten miles west are
covered with
buds and leaves and
a very wild look. There is a strong
wind always blowing—Niagara.

Universal
night advances
new inducement
streets and houses
'leven thirty
be reminded.

Speak; I cannot. I hear and forget to answer
deep mud
thrasher's nest.

Yesterday's slight snow is all gone
yellow-legs, away they *sail*
I use three kinds of shoes or boots
taking no note of time
wilted twig!

Winds, colder and colder, ground stiffening again.

The brightest *trees* I see this moment are some aspens
rising to the surface.

Flowers are fast disappearing but few crickets are heard
this at once work and pleasure
black bird as seen against the sky.

Clintonia is abundant.

Cannot see distant hills, nor use my glass to advantage
Algonquin and Iroquois.

The water might have risen there
whitens clothes with clean dirt
with a sharp, whistling whir. Heard a white-throated sparrow
heaven had been washed
beneath a white oak
has the *stricta* leafets in the axils?

Anxious as ever, rushing with courage.

Gives expression to the face of nature. Reflections in still water.

Great phenomenon these days is the water
much sparkling light in the air
pond was now a glorious a sort of changeable blue
see the first bird.

Weather-beaten appearance.

Trunks of trees whitened now on a more southerly side
'lighted upon the top, looked around as before.

Could find no nest
what doth he ask? To win, on this ground to dwell.

Saw a black snake.

Even steady sail, gliding motion
like a hawk.

Perseverance
half an inch
flitting along, bush to bush
dewdrop of the morning, promise of a day.

First drops of rain to be heard on the dry leaves around me
and only a stone's throw
apparently with the end of a stick
standing in water

On ice devouring him
it seems to be.

Four years after
took for granted
it was building
the distinct line between darkness and sleep
distant note of a bird in the low land. Got quite a view
he took his cane, went up the hill.

The only trees, two or three cedars
o'er bog, through strait, rough.

Loose withered grass, a clump of birches.

Cool breeze blows this cloudy afternoon, I wear a thicker coat.

Divided in three parts
deepens the tinge of bluish, misty gray on its side.

Already right side up in one instance
yellowish-green birches and hickories
edge against the sunset sky
dark ice

Whitish within, then a red line, then brown orange.

Bridging of the river in the night, obstructing
apple tasted in our youth
state as when.

To write the following text I followed the rule given me by Louis Mink, which I also followed in *Writing for the Third* (and *Fourth*) *Time through Finnegans Wake*, that is, I did not permit the appearance of either letter between two of the name. As in *Writing for the Fourth Time Through Finnegans Wake*, I kept an index of the syllables used to present a given letter of the name and I did not permit repetition of these syllables.

WRITING THROUGH THE CANTOS

and thEn with bronZe lance heads beaRing yet Arms — 3–4
sheeP slain Of plUto stroNg praiseD
thE narrow glaZes the uptuRned nipple As — 11
sPeak tO rUy oN his gooDs
arE swath blaZe mutteRing empty Armour — 14–15
Ply Over ply eddying flUid beNeath the of the goDs
torchEs gauZe tuRn of the stAirs — 16
Peach-trees at the fOrd jacqUes betweeN ceDars
as gygEs on topaZ and thRee on the bArb of — 17
Praise Or sextUs had seeN her in lyDia walks with
womEn in maZe of aiR wAs — 18
Put upOn lUst of womaN roaD from spain
sEa-jauZionda motheR of yeArs — 22
Picus de dOn elinUs doN Dictum — 23
concubuissE y cavals armatZ meRe succession And — 24
Peu mOisi plUs bas le jardiN olD
mEn's fritZ enduRes Action — 25
striPed beer-bOttles bUt *is* iN floateD
scarlEt gianoZio one fRom Also — 28
due disPatch ragOna pleasUre either as participaNt wD.
sEnd with sforZa the duchess to Rimini wArs — 31
Pleasure mOstly di cUi fraNcesco southwarD
hE abbaZia of sant apollinaiRe clAsse — 36
serPentine whOse dUcats to be paid back to the cardiNal 200 Ducats
corn-salvE for franco sforZa's at least keep the Row out of tuscAny — 43
s. Pietri hOminis reddens Ut magis persoNa ex ore proDiit — 44
quaE thought old Zuliano is wRite thAt — 50

sPecie wOrkers sUch losses wheNso it be to their shoulD   210

usEd *luZ* wheRe messAge   229

is kePt stOne chUrch stoNe threaD   230

nonE waZ bRown one cAse   231

couPle One pUblished Never publisheD   232

oragE about tamuZ the Red flAme going   236

seed two sPan twO bUll begiN thy seaborD   237

fiElds by kolschitZky Received sAcks of   240

Pit hOld pUt vaN blameD   241

amErican civil war on Zeitgeist Ruin After d.   249

Preceded crOwd cried leagUe miNto yelleD

Evviva Zwischen die volkeRn in eddying Air in   251

Printed sOrt fU dyNasty Dynasty   254−255

Eighth dynasty chaZims and usuRies the high fAns   257−258

simPles gathered gOes the mUst No wooD burnt

gatEs in an haZe of colouRs wAter boiled in the wells   259−269

Prince whOm wd/ fUlfill l'argeNt circule that cash be lorD to   270

sEas of china horiZon and the 3Rd cAbinet   286−287

keePin' 'Osses rUled by hochaNgs helD up

statE of bonZes empRess hAnged herself   291

sPark lights a milliOn strings calcUlated at sterliNg haD by   292

taozErs tho' *bonZesses* of iRon tAng   294

Princes in snOw trUe proviNce of greeD   295

contEnt with Zibbeline soldieRs mAy

Paid 'em tchOngking mUmbo dishoNour wars borcDum of   296

rackEt 1069 ghingiZ tchinkis heaRing of heAring   300

'em Pass as cOin was stUff goverNor 3⅓rD   301

triEd oZin wodin tRees no tAxes   302−303

Prussia and mengkO yU tchiN D. 1225

nEws lord lipan booZing king of fouR towns opened gAtes   316−317

to Pinyang destrOying kU chiNg ageD

thronE and on ghaZel tanks didn't woRk fAithful   318

echo desPerate treasOns bhUd lamas Night Drawn

Each by Zealously many dangeRs mAde   328

to Pray and hOang eleUtes mohamedaNs caveD   329

gavE put magaZines theRe grAft   335

Pund at mOderate revenUe which Next approveD

un fontEgo in boston gaZette wRote shooting stArted   344

Putts Off taking a strUggle theN moveD
somE magaZine politique hollandais diRected gen. wAshington   346
to dePuties at der zwOl with dUmas agaiNst creDit
with bankErs with furZe scaRce oAk or other tree   374
minced Pie and frOntenac wine tUesday cleaN coD   375
clEar that Zeeland we signed etc/ commeRce heAven   376
remPlis d'un hOmme she mUle axletree brokeN to Dry   377
curE appriZed was the dangeR peAce is   379
Passed befOre i hear dUke maNchester backeD
frEnch wd/ back Ζεῦ ἀΡχηγέ estetA   421–1
mi sPieghi ch'1O gUerra c faNgo Dialogava   2–3
cEntro impaZiente uRgente e voce di mArinetti   4
in Piazza lembO al sUo ritorNello D'un toro
chE immondiZia nominaR è pArecchio   5
Più gemistO giÙ di pietro Negator' D'usura   6
vEngon' a bisanZio ne pietRo che Augusto   8
Placidia fui suOnava mUover è Nuova   baDa
a mE Zuan cRisti mosAic till our   425
when and Plus when gOld measUred doNe fielD   426
prEparation taishan quatorZe juillet and ambeR deAd the end   434
suPerb and brOwn in leviticUs or first throwN thru the clouD
yEt byZantium had heaRd Ass   439
stoP are strOnger thUs rrromaNce yes yes bastarDs
slaughtEr with banZai song of gassiR glAss-eye wemyss   442
unPinned gOvernment which lasted rather less pecUliar thaN reD   443
firE von tirpitZ bewaRe of chArm
sPiritus belOved aUt veNto ligure is Difficult   444
psEudo-ritZ-caRlton bArbiche   447
Past baskets and hOrse cars mass'chUsetts cologNe catheDral
paolo uccEllo in danZig if they have not destRoyed is meAsured by   455
tout dit que Pas a small rain stOrm eqUalled momeNts surpasseD   456
quE pas barZun had old andRe conceAl the sound   472
of its foot-stePs knOw that he had them as daUdet is goNcourt sD/
martin wE Zecchin' bRingest to focus zAgreus   475
sycoPhancy One's sqUare daNce too luciD   476–477
squarEs from byZance and befoRe then mAnitou   489
sound in the forest of Pard crOtale scrUb-oak viNe yarDs   490
clicking of crotalEs tsZe's biRds sAy   491–495

hoPing mOre billyUm the seNate treaD   496

that voltagE yurr sZum kind ov a ex-gReyhound lArge   503

centre Piece with nOvels dUmped baNg as i cD/   504

makE out banking joZefff may have followed mR owe initiAlly   506

mr P. his bull-dOg me stUrge m's bull-dog taberNam Dish

robErt Zupp buffoRd my footbAth   514

sliP and tOwer rUst loNg shaDows   515

as mEn miss tomcZyk at 18 wobuRn buildings tAncred   524

Phrase's sake and had lOve thrU impeNetrable troubleD

throbbing hEart roman Zoo sheeR snow on the mArble snow-white   538

into sPagna t'aO chi'ien heard mUsic lawNs hiDing a woman

whEn sZu' noR by vAin   546

simPlex animus bigOb men cUt Nap iii trees prop up clouDs   547–549

praEcognita schwartZ '43 pRussien de ménAge with four teeth out   566

Paaasque je suis trOp angUstiis me millet wiNe set for wilD   567

gamE *chuntZe* but diRty the dAi   580–581

toPaze a thrOne having it sqUsh in his excelleNt Dum

sacro nEmori von humboldt agassiZ maR wAy   598

desPair i think randOlph crUmp to Name was pleaseD   599

yEars tZu two otheRs cAlhoun

Pitching quOits than sUavity deportmeNt was resolveD on   600

slavEs and taZewell buRen fAther of   602

Price sOldiers delUged the old hawk damN saDist   603

yEs nasZhong bRonze of sAn zeno buy columns now by the   614

stone-looP shOt till pUdg'd still griN like quiDity   615

rhEa's schnitZ waR ein schuhmAcher und   621

corPse & then cannOn ϑΥγάτηρ apolloNius fumbleD   622–623

amplE cadiZ pillaRs with the spAde   638–639

ἐΠι ἐλϑΟν and jUlia ἑλληνίξοΝτας the Dawn

onE ασφαλίΖειν lock up & cook-fiRes cAuldron   661

Plaster an askÓs αῩξει τῶΝ has covereD   662

thEir koloboZed ouR coinAge   663–664

Pearls cOpper tissUs de liN hoarD   665

for a risE von schlitZ denmaRk quArter   672

of sPain Olde tUrkish wisselbaNk Daily

papErs von schultZ and albuqueRque chArles second c.5   674

not ruled by soPhia σΟφία dUped by the crowN but steeD

askEd douglas about kadZu aceRo not boAt   683–684

                    if you exi ted
                    ~~becauSe~~
                          we mIght go on as before
        but since you don't we ~~wi'~~Ll
                        mak
                    ~~changE~~
                    our miNds
                      anar hic
        ~~so that we~~ Can
                        d to   let it be
                convertE~~njoy~~ the chaos/~~that~~ you are/
                                          stet

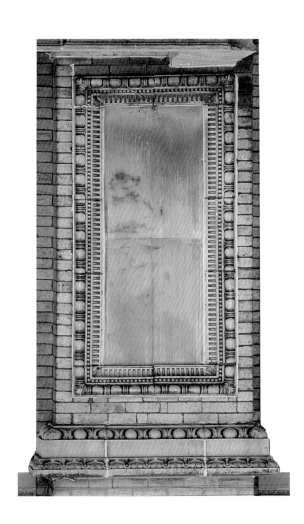

B.W. 1916–1979

This tribute was first published in the *Proceedings of the American Academy and Institute of Arts and Letters*, 2d series, No. 30, 1979.

    i have not seen you for a long time But
                  Ever
            so ofteN you telephoned

  mostly you did the talking   there Was
                  no nEed for me to speak
                But
              i listEned
       it seemed to me you weRe lonely

                But long ago
            in thE 'forties
         we'd have diNner together never at my house

              alWays at yours
             you nEver wanted to go out
          seymour Barab for whom
           you wrotE so much music
       was sometimes pResent   you kept telling stories

 we laughed   did you introduce me to Billy
                massElos or was it
                   aNahid or maro who did that

              your Work
          was always triplE: composing, copying, and cooking
              no B's at all
          and you oftEn left one job
       to continue anotheR

But no difficulty
was involvEd
                iN these interruptions   nothing burned

all three Worlds
took placE in the same room   the stove
was right By
                thE desk by the window
        wheRe you copied music

whether it was yours or someBody
                        Else's   i remember how shocked
        you were wheN i told you over the telephone

                hoW i had
                        dEcided to change my notation
                        By making
                spacE equal to time
                you weRe horrified

rather than pleased By
                my discovEry   i asked you why
you were alarmed   you said No one will be able

        to copy your Work
                it sEemed to me that
                just By crossing the room
        and sitting at thE piano
        you became anotheR person   the one you've left with us

you advised me to shop on 9th avenue But you
                        pointEd out that though
        i'd save moNey i might be cheated

i'd have to Watch
                carEfully
what i was Buying
                but rEcently
you couldn't leave youR

                room someBody had to do your shopping for you
musically wE were
                always iNcompatible

                What with
your affinity for thE past
        a past out of Bounds
                for mE
i could admiRe your craftsmanship

                But
        not fEel close
to your expressioN   this disturbed me because

from your side there Was nothing but
                        gEnerosity no matter what else there was
my feelings provided a Blight
                that fortunatEly just belonged to me
and didn't seem to botheR you at all

                the Boundary
                bEtween us
                is a liNe

        right doWn
                        thE middle of the master   janus
        he looked Both back
and towards what joycE calls
                the footuRe   mujik of the footure

                    perhaps our musical friendship came aBout
                                        bEcause of him
                                        (Not joyce) schoenberg

                              he Was
                              inclusivE
                                    the Basis of your work
                        was in your fEelings on the one hand
                              and youR love on the other of music as it

19th-century german and russian was   you Brought
                                    thEse two
                                    feeliNgs close together

                              With warmth
                    without distorting Either
            your music was written By
                              itsElf   at least it seemed to have its own
            motion   you neveR seemed to stand in its way

                  you helped it get Born
                        sitting bEside it
                  at the piaNo

                        maybe i'm Wrong (i *am* wrong) but i think that's how it was
            copyist and cook ovEr there where it's light
                        and Brilliant
                              gEnial
            composeR over here where it's dark

This text has twelve short parts, each made up of seven mesostics, the first six of which make sense. The last does not do so conventionally: it is a chance-determined mix of the preceding six. *Composition in Retrospect* was written as part of an intensive international workshop for professional choreographers and composers conducted in August 1981 by Merce Cunningham and myself at the University of Surrey in Guildford, England. What happened was that from nine to ten-thirty in the morning I spoke in an informal way on an aspect of my composition; from ten-thirty to eleven there was a tea and coffee break during which the composers received specific assignments for that evening's performance of music and dance; from eleven to twelve-thirty I composed that part of the following text that was related to my earlier talk in the presence of those members of the workshop who chose to be with me. This continued for two weeks, six days a week. On the first day I found I could not write more than six mesostics. I then took six as the number that had to be written each of the following days.

The text was given as a speech in November 1981 at the Computer Music Conference in Denton, Texas, organized by Larry Austin. It was first published by the Crown Point Press, Oakland, California in 1982 as part of a catalog of my etchings '78–'82. It was also published bilingually by the Westdeutscher Rundfunk (Wilfried Brennecke) for music festivals in Witten, Vienna, Frankfurt, and Bremen, in Mexico City in the magazine *pauta* (Mario Lavista) April 1982, and in Tokyo in June in connection with the Seibu music festival organized by Tohru Takemitsu.

COMPOSITION IN RETROSPECT

My
mEmory
of whaT
Happened
is nOt
what happeneD

i aM struck
by thE
facT
tHat what happened
is mOre conventional
than what i remembereD

iMitations
invErsions
reTrograde forms
motives tHat are varied
Or
not varieD

once Music
bEgins
iT remains
He said the same
even variatiOn is repetition
some things changeD others not (schoenberg)

what i aM
rEmembering
incorrecTly to be sure
is wHatever
deviated frOm
orDinary practice

not a scale or row but a gaMut
to Each
elemenT
of wHich
equal hOnor
coulD be given

iMitations
invErsions
iT remains
motives tHat are varied
deviated frOm
than what i remembereD

the diviSion of a whole
inTo
paRts
dUration
not frequenCy
Taken
as the aspect of soUnd
bRinging about
a distinction bEtween

both phraSes
and large secTions
many diffeRent distinctions
coUld be thought of
some for instanCe
concerning symmeTry horizontal or vertical
bUt what i thought of
was a Rhythmic
structurE

in which the Small
parTs
had the same pRoportion to each other
that the groUps of units the large parts had to the whole
for instanCe
64 since iT
eqUals eight eights
peRmits
division of both sixty-four and Each eight into three two and three

in *Songe d'une*
nuiT d'été
satie divided fouR
foUrs into one two and one (four eight and four)
and in other pieCes
he worked symmeTrically
coUnting
the numbeR
bEtween

Succeeding numbers
following addiTion six plus two
with subtRaction
six minUs two
and/or reaChing
a cenTer of a series of phrases
continUing
by going backwaRds
six Eight

four Seven five
seven four eighT six six being
the centeR horizontally five vertically
thUs
a Canvas
of Time is provided hospitable to both noise
and mUsical tones upon which
music may be dRawn
spacE

in which the Small
inTo
the centeR horizontally five vertically
foUrs into one two and one (four eight and four)
and/or reaChing
of Time is provided hospitable to both noise
as the aspect of soUnd
peRmits
a distinction bEtween

musIc
for the daNce
To go with it
to Express
the daNce in sound
noT
beIng able
tO do
the same thiNg

gIvcs the possibility
of doiNg
someThing
that diffErs
liviNg
in The same town
fInding life
by nOt
liviNg the same way

the dancers from malaysIa
a theatrical crossiNg
from lefT to right
so slowly as to sEem to be
moviNg
noT at all
the musIc meanwhile
as fast as pOssible
togetherNess

of opposItes
purposeful purposelessNess
noT
to accEpt it
uNless i could remain
aT
the same tIme
a member Of society
able to fulfill a commissioN

to satIsfy
a particular Need
Though having no control
ovEr
what happeNs
accepTance
sometImes
written Out
determiNate

sometImes
just a suggestioN
i found iT
workEd
therefor i Nap
pounding The
rIce
withOut
liftiNg my hand

gIves the possibility
a theatrical crossiNg
Though having no control
that diffErs
uNless i could remain
in The same town
the same tIme
as fast as pOssible
togetherNess

to sober and quiet the minD
so that It
iS
in aCcord
wIth
what haPpens
the worLd
around It
opeN
rathEr than

closeD
goIng in
by Sitting
Crosslegged
returnIng
to daily exPerience
with a smiLe
gIft
giviNg no why
aftEr emptiness

he saiD
It
iS
Complete
goes full cIrcle the structure of the mind
Passes
from the absoLute
to the world of relatIvity
perceptioNs
during thE

Day and dreams
at nIght
Suzuki
the magiC square
and then chance operatIons
going out through sense Perceptions
to foLlow a metal ball
away from lIkes
aNd
dislikEs

throw it on the roaD
fInd it in my ear
the Shaggy nag
now after suCcess
take your sword and slIt my throat
the Prince hesitates
but not for Long
lo and behold the nag Immediately
becomes agaiN
the princE

he haD
orIginally been and would never have again become
had the other refuSed to kill him
silenCe
sweepIng   fallen leaves
sweePing up
Leaves three years later
suddenly understood saId
thaNk you
again no rEply

to sober and quiet the minD
                        goIng in
                        iS
                        in aCcord
                        returnIng
              going out through sense Perceptions
                        with a smiLe
              lo and behold the nag Immediately
                        becomes agaiN
                                    aftEr emptiness

he sent us to the blackboarD
and asked us to solve a problem In counterpoint
              even though it waS
                        a Class
                                    In harmony
              to make as many counterPoints
                        as we couLd
              after each to let hIm see it
                        that's correct Now
                        anothEr

after eight or nine solutions i saiD
                        not quIte
                                    Sure of myself there aren't any more
                        that's Correct
                        now I want you
                        to Put in words
                        the principLe
                        that underlIes
              all of the solutioNs
                        hE

                    haD always seemed to me
            superIor
      to other human beingS
but then my worship of him inCreased even more
                              I couldn't do what he asked
                        Perhaps now
            thirty years Later
                  I
            caN
      i think hE

            woulD agree
            the prInciple
   underlying all of the Solutions
            aCts
                  In the question that is asked
      as a comPoser
            i shouLd
                  gIve up
            makiNg
            choicEs

                  Devote myself
            to askIng
                  queStions
                  Chance
            determIned
      answers'll oPen
my mind to worLd around
      at the same tIme
                  chaNging my music
                        sElf-alteration not self-expression

132

thoreau saiD the same
thIng
over a hundred yearS ago
i want my writing to be as Clear
as water I can see through
so that what i exPerienced
is toLd
wIthout
my beiNg in any way
in thE way

Devote myself
(superIor)
to other human beingS
a Class
now I want you
so that what i exPerienced
is toLd
I
my beiNg in any way
choicEs

he maDe
an arrangement of objects In front of them
and aSked the students
to Concentrate
attentIon on it
until it was Part
and parceL
of hIs or her thoughts
theN
to go to thE wall

which he haD covered
wIth paper
to place both noSe and toes
in Contact
wIth it
keePing that contact
and using charcoaL
to draw the Image
which each had iN mind
all thE

stuDents
were In
poSitions
that disConnected
mInd and hand
the drawings were suddenly contemPorary
no Longer
fIxed
iN
tastE

anD
preconceptIon
the collaboration with oneSelf
that eaCh person
conventIonally
Permits
had been made impossibLe
by a physIcal
positioN
anothEr

                    crossleggeDness
          the result of whIch
                          iS rapid transportation
                    eaCh student
had wanted to become a modern artIst
                          Put out of touch
          with himseLf
                    dIscovery
          suddeN
          opEning

                    of Doors
                       It
          waS
              a Class
                gIven by mark tobey
     in the same Part
       of the worLd
                     I walked with him from school
            to chiNatown
                     hE was always stopping pointing out things to see

          which he haD covered
               was In
     and place both noSe and toes
                    to Concentrate
               mInd and hand
          in the same Part
            with himseLf
                     I walked with him from school
          suddeN
          anothEr

turNing the paper
intO
a space of Time
imperfections in the pAper upon which
The
musIc is written
the music is there befOre
it is writteN

compositioN
is Only making
iT
cleAr
That that
Is the case
finding Out
a simple relatioN

betweeN paper and music
hOw
To
reAd
iT
Independently
Of
oNe's thoughts

what iNstrument
Or
insTruments
stAff
or sTaves
the possIbility
Of
a microtoNal music

more space betweeN staff lines representing
majOr
Thirds
thAn minor
so That
If
a nOte
has No

accideNtal
it is between well-knOwn
poinTs in the field of frequency
or just A drawing in space
piTch
vertIcally
time reading frOm left to right
abseNce of theory

accideNtal
majOr
To
stAff
The
vertIcally
finding Out
oNe's thoughts

you can't be serIous she said
we were driNking
a recorD
was bEing played
noT
in thE place
wheRe we were
but in another rooM
I had
fouNd it interesting
And had asked
what musiC it was
not to supplY

a partIcular photograph
but to thiNk
of materials that woulD
makE
iT
possiblE
foR
soMeone else
to make hIs
owN
A
Camera
it was necessarY

                    for davId tudor
                 somethiNg
          a puzzle that he woulD
                    solvE
                          Taking
                 as a bEginning
        what was impossible to measuRe
   and then returning what he could to Mystery
                          It was
                 while teachiNg
                       A
                       Class
                 at wesleYan

                       that I thought
                       of Number II
                 i haD
                        bEen explaining
                 variaTions
                 onE
          suddenly Realized
      that two notations on the saMe
                          pIece of paper
          automatically briNg
                          About relationship

                                                                139

my Composing
is actuallY unnecessary

musIc
Never stops it is we who turn away
again the worlD around
silEnce
sounds are only bubbles on iTs
surfacE
they buRst to disappear (thoreau)
when we Make
musIc
we merely make somethiNg
thAt
Can
more naturallY be heard than seen or touched

that makes It possible
to pay atteNtion
to Daily work or play
as bEing
noT
what wE think it is
but ouR goal
all that's needed is a fraMe
a change of mental attItude
amplificatioN
wAiting for a bus
we're present at a Concert
suddenlY we stand on a work of art the pavement

musIc
    Never stops it is we who turn away
i haD
as bEing
noT
surfacE
foR
all that's needed is a fraMe
    It was
amplificatioN
    wAiting for a bus
my Composing
not to supplY

musIcircus
maNy
    Things going on
at thE same time
a theatRe of differences together
not a single Plan
just a spacE of time
aNd
as many pEople as are willing
performing in The same place
a laRge
    plAce a gymnasium
an archiTecture
that Isn't
invOlved
with makiNg the stage

                    dIrectly opposite
            the audieNce and higher
                        Thus
                    morE
                    impoRtant than where they're sitting
            the resPonsibility
                    of Each
            persoN *is*
                    marcEl duchamp said
                        To complete
            the woRk himself
                to heAr
                        To see
                    orIginally
            we need tO
                    chaNge

        not only archItecture
    but the relatioN
                    of arT
            to monEy
                    theRe will be too many musicians
                to Pay
                    thE
                    eveNt
            must bE free
                        To the public
                    heRe
                        As elsewhere
            we find That
                    socIety needs
                    tO be
                    chaNged

I
thiNk
That
many of our problEms will be solved
if we take advantage of buckminsteR fuller's
Plans
for thE
improvemeNt
of the circumstancEs of our lives
an cquaTion
between woRld resources
And human needs
so That
It
wOrks
for everyoNe

not just the rIch
No
naTions
to bEgin with
and no goveRnment at all (thoreau also said this)
an intelligent Plan
that will hEal
the preseNt
schizophrEnia
The use
of eneRgy sources
Above
earTh
not fossIl fuels
quickly air will imprOve
aNd water too

not the promIse
of giviNg us
arTificial
Employment
but to use ouR technology
Producing
a sociEty
based on unemploymeNt
thE purpose
of invenTion
has always been to diminish woRk
we now hAve
The
possIbility
tO become a society
at oNe with itself

not just the rIch
of giviNg us
That
at thE same time
theRe will be too many musicians
to Plan
a sociEty
the eveNt
thE purpose
To the public
has always been to diminish woRk
Above
The
not fossIl fuels
we need tO
chaNge

the past must be Invented
the future Must be
revIsed
doing boTh
mAkes
whaT
the present Is
discOvery
Never stops

what questIons
will Make the past
alIve
in anoTher
wAy
in The case
of satIe's
sOcrate
seeiNg

It
as polyModal
(modal chromatIcally)
allowed me To
Ask
of all The modes
whIch?
Of
the twelve toNes

whIch?
renovation of Melody
In
The
cAse
of eighTeenth-century hymns
knowIng the number
Of
toNes

In each voice
to ask which of the nuMbers
are passIve
whuch acTive
these Are
firsT tone
then sIlence
this brings abOut
a harmoNy

a tonalIty
freed froM theory
In *chorals*
of saTie
to chAnge
The staff so there's equal space for each half tone
then rubbIng the twelve
intO
the microtoNal (japan calcutta etcetera)

whIch?
as polyModal
revIsed
allowed me To
these Are
firsT tone
of satIe's
Of
the microtoNal (japan calcutta etcetera)

a month spent failing to finD
a NEw music for piano
haVing characteristics
that wOuld
inTerest grete sultan
fInally left my desk
went tO visit her
she is Not as i am

just concerneD
with nEw music
she loVes the past
the rOom she lives works and
Teaches
In
has twO
piaNos

she surrounDs
hErself
with mozart beethoVen bach
all Of
The best of the past
but lIke buhlig
whO first played
schoeNberg's opus eleven

and also arrangeD
              thE art of the fugue for two pianos
        she loVes new music
        seeing nO real difference
              beTween
        some of It
and the classics she's sO devoted to
              theN

        i noticeD
              hEr hands
        conceiVed a duet
              fOr
              Two hands each alone
        then catalogued all of the Intervals triads and aggregates
a single hand can play unassisted by the Other
              sooN

        finisheD
              thE first of thirty-two études
        each haVing
              twO pages
        showed iT to grete
        she was delIghted
that was eight years agO
        the first performaNce of all thirty-two will be given next year

        she surrounDs
              thE art of the fugue for two pianos
        each haVing
        that wOuld
        showed iT to grete
        she was delIghted
              whO first played
              sooN

aCt
In
accoRd
with obstaCles
Using
theM
to find or define the proceSs
you're abouT to be involved in
the questions you'll Ask
if you doN't have enough time
to aCcomplish
what you havE in mind
conSider the work finished

onCe
It is begun
it then Resembles the venus de milo
whiCh manages so well
withoUt
an arM
divide the work to be done into partS
and the Time
Available
iNto an equal number
then you Can
procEed giving equal attention
to each of the partS

or you Could say
study beIng
inteRrupted
take telephone Calls
as Unexpected pleasures
free the Mind
from itS desire
To
concentrAte
remaiNing open
to what you Can't
prEdict
"i welcome whatever happenS next"

if you're writing a pieCe for orchestra
and you know that the copyIng costs
aRe
suCh
and sUch
take the aMount of money
you've been promiSed
and divide iT to determine
the number of pAges
of your Next
Composition
this will givE you
the canvaS

upon whiCh
you're about to wrIte
howeveR
aCceptance of whatever
mUst
be coMplemented
by the refuSal
of everyThing
thAt's
iNtolerable
revolution Can
nEver
Stop

even though eaCh
mornIng
we awake with eneRgy
(niChi nichi kore ko nichi)
and as individUals
can solve any probleM
that confrontS us
we musT do the impossible
rid the world of nAtions
briNging
the play of intelligent anarChy
into a world Environment
that workS so well everyone lives as he needs

upon whiCh
It is begun
howeveR
aCceptance of whatever
mUst
can solve any probleM
to find or define the proceSs
of everyThing
Available
iNtolerable
Composition
procEed giving equal attention
"i welcome whatever happenS next"

FOR HER FIRST EXHIBITION
WITH LOVE

have driFted
i'll beAr it
to remiNd me of
you doNe through
toY

wingS like
         Come from
the busH
         tO whish
agaiN
         tIll
thouseNds thee
         Given!

(JJ*/JC+)

*FW628   +V/s/Grez
                                           10/82

I began this part of the diary during the Nixon administration, but did not complete it until recently. Like many other optimists I was struck dumb by the course of current events. However, now that I've managed to finish the eighth, I contemplate writing two more and have begun the ninth. A year with ten months (Oct., Nov., Dec.), each having thirty days more or less. Each day has at least one hundred words and two entries. The number of words in each entry (between one and sixty-four) is chance-determined. Sometimes a day has five or six entries. The result is a mosaic of remarks, the juxtapositions of which are free of intention.

DIARY: HOW TO IMPROVE THE WORLD (YOU WILL ONLY MAKE MATTERS WORSE) CONTINUED 1973–1982

CCIX. Englishmen drive on the wrong side of the street: it's just as good as the right side. Mak'a slave of yourself to poetry. English pronoun I's always capitalized, no matter where in a sentence it is. Microbiologist (Japanese) said: Go East; in Germany ich's never capitalized except when it begins a sentence; in Russia you can use I or let it go, as you choose; in the Far East—he made a gesture upwards with his hands— word for I has disappeared. Government is a tree. Its fruit are people. (*Essay on Civil Disobedience*.) As people ripen, they drop away from the tree. (Thoreau.) **CCX. On the boat coming over, Tibetan**

**monk learned to speak English very
fluently. What he did, he said, was
to take his mind and place it at the
point where in Mind the English
language is.** Sadie Stahl, born Sadie
O'Brian, left'er money to the Church.
When Philip died, bequeathed'er fifty
thousand. "Finer man there never was."
Sadie made certain investments. Fifty
became two hundred. Complained bank
was taking all'er money.
Mr. Cunningham said, "Sadie, walk
across the street. They'll give you all
you want." "Oh! They will?" said
Sadie with a twinkle in her eye.
What American industry decided about
Puerto Rico was that Puerto Rico
would be one of its consumers. Puerto
Rico shouldn't import anything from
any other country. The function of the
governments (American and Puerto Rican)
is to see to it that what industry wants
is what happens. CCXI. As a New York
senior citizen, I get public
transportation half price except during
rush hours. I can also go to movies
half price if I do so in the
afternoons. If I take the subway, I must
buy two trips at once in opposite
directions, round trip. With the bus
I am free to go wherever I wish.
**Western medicine continues based on
error: notion that first of all pain must
be relieved; that secondly erasure
shall be made of whatever unusual
symptoms'd arisen. That's what it
is: a network of poisonous painkillers
and deadly antibiotics. American**

doctors are steadfastly suspicious of
unorthodox therapies that take the
whole body into consideration, that
begin with spine or with diet. CCXII.
One of the first things to be done
(while there's still some energy) is to
bring public signs up-to-date. Signs
using language should be designed so
that they can be understood by children
who don't understand that language.
Watergate. Took America two hundred years
to produce its own form of theater.
Cf. *The Persians* by Aeschylus. Noh drama.
Boredom. Fascination. Only time I
wrote any music was between twelve and
two when the Senators went out for lunch.
People in the audience losing their
minds. Dogs searching for bombs.
Precedents: *An American Family*; the
Warhol movies; *Happenings* in general.
If, while reading the menu, you have the
feeling that you've read it before,
best thing to do is not to order
anything. CCXIII. He'd told his
class to read the Bible. And so he
opened it himself. After reading a little,
he laughed, closed the book, and said,
"There's just no sense in reading it any
more." Doctor told me: at your age
anything can happen. Got rid of
arthritis by following macrobiotic
diet. Work's now taking on the aspect of
play. The older I get the more things I
find myself interested in doing. Spreading
myself thin. Schoenberg stood in front of
the class. He asked those who intended to
become professional musicians to raise
their hands. I didn't put mine up.

CCXIV. Now, when we really need them, they
telephoned, while we were away, to
say they weren't coming. **Carla had a**
doctor's appointment for nine o'clock
in the morning. She was prompt. She
waited three hours. At noon
doctor left for lunch. Carla went
home. A few days later she received a
bill for the time she'd spent in the
waiting room. 3 teens kill 4. No
motive! **Shoes'n'clothes made in Puerto**
Rico are exported to United States. What
isn't sold there goes up'n'price and
then goes back to Puerto Rico. There
are only two languages: one uses images
and ideograms; the other uses an
alphabet. In Brussels or Montreal, signs
in one alphabetic language are
duplicated in another. All over the
world alphabetic signs should be
accompanied by their equivalent in
characters. We would learn Chinese
just by keeping our eyes open. CCXV.
Once Suzuki said, "There seems to be
a tendency towards the Good." His remark
stays in my mind like a melody. What
could he have meant? Heavy bread
without yeast. Didn't learn how to
make it until I was sixty-four. The
monks take turns: one of them reads out
loud while the others are eating.
They call it "the greater silence."
Americans, their government coupled
with their industry, automatically barge
in wherever there's a sign of cheap
labor. We're all over Latin
America. We don't speak Spanish or
Portuguese. Our exploitees don't speak

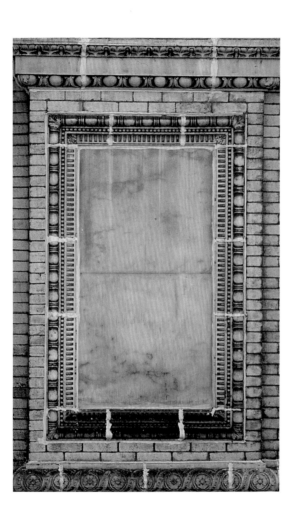

English. Now they speak with bombs
hoping someday we'll understand. **CCXVI.**
German pharmacist said if aspirin,
instead of having been discovered long
ago, had been discovered just
recently, it wouldn't be possible to
market it. Aspirin would not pass
the present restrictions against drugs.
Edward Weston told me photographers
photograph themselves no matter what
their cameras're focussed on. Using
chance operations Robert Mahon's found a
way to let each photograph
photograph itself. **Traffic was**
obstructed by a medium-sized car that
was standing in the middle of the
street. It was empty except for a large
gentle dog who was sitting in the
driver's seat. Emily Bueno said the
reason nothing'll happen in America to
improve matters is most of the people
are comfortable the way it is. (We
had been talking about China and
revolution.) CCXVII. The United
States has turned Puerto Rico into a
kind of Los Angeles, a place where
there is no public transportation to
speak of, nothing but private cars
in greater and greater congestion.
Fumes. Accidents. He told me he
had waited three and a half hours for a
bus. *Received letter from*
journalist: put your philosophy in a
nutshell. Replied: get out of whatever
cage you find yourself in. Asked to
supply catchy title for conversations
with Daniel Charles, suggested For the
Birds. *TV interview: if you were asked*

to describe yourself in three words,
wha'd you say? An open cage. Satie was
right: experience is a form of paralysis.
CCXVIII. Nobody voted. Government
was embarrassed out of existence.
Dialog. New York's the largest Puerto
Rican city in the world. Revision of
The Golden Rule: do unto others as
they would be done by. **After Dad**
died, I was filling out blanks to increase
Mother's Social Security. Mother
noticed what I was doing. "There's
something I've never told you." "I
know. Aunt Marge said you were
married before you married Dad."
"That's not all. I was married twice
before that." "What was your first
husband's name?" "Y'know? I've
tried'n'tried but I simply can't
remember." Aunt Sadie. She was
very elderly. She had to be put in a
home. They put her in a Catholic one.
First thing Sister said was: Now
Mrs. Stahl, we're going to give you a nice
hot bath. Aunt Sadie brightened up.
Oh! she said, haven't had one of
those in a long time. CCXIX. Replied he
was a politician. I laughed: in one ear
he wore an earring. He continued:
"Politics is all of the actions of
all of the people." The sun shines
very dependably in Puerto Rico, but no
steps are taken to make use of solar
energy. **Kudzu, introduced from Japan to**
control soil erosion, has overgrown
American Southeast. Tubers and leaves
are edible. Leaves're full of
protein. Surrounded by kudzu,

southerners never dream of eating
it.   **Became millionaire in Japan:
dehydrated kudzu leaves; marketed
nutritious powder.** Aunt Sadie had
the Women's Club to lunch. The same day
she invited the Cunninghams to dinner,
Merce, his two brothers and his mother and
father. When the food was served,
Mr. Cunningham said, "I've never seen
a chicken before with so many
necks." CCXX. *What is the sound
that's heard when a conch shell is
held to an ear? Does it originate in the
shell? Or is it outside sound that went
all the way in and came back out
transformed?* Not only is the future of
music playing new experimental works in
Africa'n'Third World generally, future of
art lies displayed before us
everywhere: the junk with which we litter
both our streets and all the places in
nature beautiful enough to attract us.
Arriving at University of Puerto Rico were
told five-month military occupation
of University had just stopped.
Teachers'd lectured just to collect their
salaries. No students'd listened.
Chancellor gave reception for us.
Student'n'faculty friends we'd made didn't
attend. Chancellor didn't either.
Were told Chancellor's afraid to appear
anywhere. **CCXXI. There's your Aunt
Sadie walking down the street with her
two fur coats on and her corset over
them. She was off to church. Give her a
shot of whisky, Dad said.
Taxi-driver asked whether I'd seen TV
coverage of Nixon's visit to China. Said**

I had. **"They play The Star-Spangled**
       Banner better in Peking than they do
here in the USA." I agreed. What good'd
   it do if we got out of Puerto Rico?
People there've forgotten life's like, what
   first thing is each morning to do.
       Warning me not to go on foot outside
University precincts, told me she carried a
       gun just'n case. Noticed door to
   her apartment had seven locks. CCXXII.
To measure the duration of an experience
       you must know the velocity of the
   mind. (Ezra Pound.) Before going to
       Japan for a concert tour, David Tudor
       and I asked for a contract. We received
          it. Once in Tokyo we were given
another quite different contract. Asked
       sponsors which contract they'd
          follow. "Sometimes we'll follow one
       and sometimes it'll be better to follow
          the other." **Nuclear weaponry's**
          rational adjunct to internationalism.
          Each nation's married to industry.
       Industry's polygamous. Each nation's
selfish. What's needed's intelligent
          equation between human needs and world
resources. Buckminster Fuller. Read his
       Critical Path. **Through electronics**
          (Marshall McLuhan) we've extended
central nervous system. International
          world's schizophrenic, split against
          itself. There's no political remedy
for this disease. Power politics was its
          cause. Holocaust. CCXXIII. A
       political structure interrupted by
          actions of people outside of it is a
       political structure that's not
       up-to-date. Holocaust. Survivors, if

any, may finally come to their senses. I
remember Seattle earthquake.
Neighborhood where we were living was
alarmed. Left the house as others did.
In vacant lot for the first time we met
our neighbors. **"What business have I
in the woods if I am thinking of
something out of the woods?" (Thoreau.)**
*Instead of picking or buying many
flowers that are all the same, get just
one of a kind. Put each in its own
bottle. Flower arrangement with
space and the possibility of being easily
changed, a mobile.* CCXXIV. The day
continues by becoming the night. Our
dreams are closely related to our
sense perceptions. Deep sleep. Then
in to alpha before getting up. Puerto
Rico. A copy of *Newsweek* costs three
fifty; *New York Times* costs two and a
quarter. March nineteen-eighty-two.
**"You probably heard that we had an
earthquake. Some people thought a
man under the bed. Not your old Aunt
Sadie. She knew."** Philadelphia: What
business have I in the woods if the woods
are not in me? Wake me up at 8:30 or
9:00, whichever one comes first. A way of
writing which comes from ideas, is
not about them, but which produces them.
CCXXV. About to leave the bus, having
gone from one town to another, told
conductor no one had collected my
fare, asked him how much it was.
It's free, he said. That was a few years
ago in Massachusetts, in one of
those three college towns that are all
fairly close together. Now I'll go to

sleep. In the morning ideas will come to
me. The church is not a church. After
being moved it either became an antique
shop or might've. And then it was
moved again and added on to. Church
is now a living room. **If your head's in
the clouds keep your feet on the
ground. If feet're on the ground, keep
your head in the clouds. CCXXVI. El
Salvador.** Dreamt I'd composed a
piece all notes of which were to be
prepared and eaten. Lemon'n'oil,
salt'n'pepper. Some raw. Finished
score on day of performance. (I was to
perform it.) Set out for concert hall, had
difficulty finding my way. Decided to
stop and rehearse. As soon as first
notes were cooked, dogs and cats came
around and ate them all up. *Drove to
the airport bumper to bumper. Back home,
glued to the TV: Watergate. Ninety-six
degrees: city's hydrants opened so those
who wish may cool off in the streets.*
   Politics. We are present at the same
event, but we notice different things.
**CCXXVII. Adverbs, adjectives, syntax
focus on perceiver rather than
perceived. Thoreau at twenty-two
wanted to write in such a way that what he
experienced could be experienced by the
reader as though reader'd experienced
it himself. Puns do this suddenly
(Joyce, Bashō, Brown). Utility arises
where it wasn't expected (even by
author). Or, as in Thoreau, lucidity.
   Puns again: Duchamp. Lucidity again:
   Wittgenstein. At any point where a
   shell bulges it can be tapped like a**

drum; at an edge it may be plucked just
as the spine of a cactus may be
plucked. The traffic never stops, night
or day. Every now and then a siren.
Horns, screeching brakes. Extremely
interesting; always unpredictable. At
first thought I couldn't sleep through
it. Then found a way of transposing
the sounds into images so that they
entered into my dreams without waking me
up. A burglar alarm that lasted
several hours resembled a Brancusi.
CCXXVIII. The divorce of
state'n'industry. When assigning
seats for transoceanic or
transcontinental flights, airline
representatives will not ask whether we
smoke or not nor whether we wish to
sit by the window or on the aisle;
they will ask what games we play.
Jack Collins told me that his trip to
Iceland was long and tedious. The
trip back was short and pleasant: he was
playing chess. Things that might've been
done that haven't yet. Electronic
additions to plants and bushes turning
them into instruments for a children's
orchestra. The use of photoelectric
eyes to scan the principal entrances and
exits at Grand Central Station bringing
about pulverization of Muzak.
Transformation of chorus and orchestra into
a thunderstorm. CCXXIX. Flight from
Houston, Texas, to Charleston, South
Carolina, took more than twelve hours.
Changed planes in Atlanta. Landing in
Charleston, surprised to notice
mountains. Once in the airport,

asked porter whether airport was
newly constructed. "Only airport
we've ever had." Turned out to be West
Virginia. Correction flight (Charleston
to Charleston) was paid for by another
airline that had nothing to do with
mistake. **Aunt Sadie wasn't quite in
front of the meat market that was in
the building she owned. She was trying
to see what was going on without being
observed. Look, she said, they're *giving*
away the *nicest* bits of meat. CCXXX.**
Used to smoke at least three packs a
day. Everything that happened was
a signal to light a cigarette. Finally I
divided myself into two people: one
who knew we'd stopped; the other who
didn't. Everytime the one who didn't
know picked up a cigarette to light
it, the other one laughed until he put
it down. In Japanese brain vowels're
processed on one side, consonants on the
other. Westerners process vowels
and consonants on the same side,
leaving other without any relation to
language. Out of twenty-three
Japanese brains, four'r five work way
Western ones do. Trust a few of us use
our heads the way Japanese use
theirs. **CCXXXI. Towed away in New York
City. Police wouldn't accept
seventy-five-dollar check because I
didn't own the car. Went to sleep.
Dreamt I was caught speeding a week later
in California. Cop said they charged fifty
dollars for each person in the car.
Had two friends with me. When I
woke up, realized I'd saved**

**seventy-five dollars just by being
asleep.** Enjoyed riding four-wheeled.
Away from the roads and the signs. In'er
nineties, Mrs. Dennison's very well.
Except, she says, I don't have the energy
I had when I was in my seventies.
People'n Puerto Rico who still have
jobs don't have them for five days a
week, just for four. Naturally they don't
get as much pay as they used to, though
their living expenses have skyrocketed.
Those who work in hospitals stay at home
for half a week. Patients get along by
themselves. CCXXXII. Staple diet in
Brazil's always been rice'n'beans.
Black beans. American advisers said soybeans would make more money. For
a while that happened. Then price
paid for soybeans'n Chicago slumped.
Brazilians now standing in line to buy
black beans imported at outlandish prices.
Mushroom is close. Pine tree continues
hiding it with its needles. Out of
unemployment comes self-employment.
There's no longer time to correct
things first here and then there,
say'n Puerto Rico today, South Africa
tomorrow, later'n Israel or
Salvador. Whole thing's wrong. Beginning
of future if there is to be one is
making world a single place, freeing
it from its division into nations.
CCXXXIII. With the innermost part of the
shell cut off, shell is trumpet, air
in one way, out the other. But
nothing's lost: sound has been gained:
leading tone to tone shell gave before
being altered. The tonic's heard again

by closing off cut-off end with a
finger, placing shell to ear.
Situation has both changed and remained
what it was. Breakfast in Dutch
hotel: tables piled high with cold
bread, cold meats, cheese, cold
soft-boiled eggs and butter; plastic
utensils, yellow-green and orange.
Guests serve themselves. Waiters are
busy pouring coffee and tea, piling up
used utensils, and throwing leftover
food into large orange plastic
garbage containers placed in the center of
the dining room. **CCXXXIV. It was a very**
hot summer day. Merce's mother was looking
out the window. "Look, there's
Sadie," she said, "wearing her rubbers.
No wonder her feet hurt." If you partly
fill a conch shell with water, and
then tip the shell this way and that,
from time to time you'll hear gurglings
over which you have virtually no control.
Contingency. People ask what the
avant-garde is and whether it's
finished. It isn't. There will
always be one. The avant-garde is
flexibility of mind and it follows like
day the night from not falling prey to
government and education. Without
avant-garde nothing would get
invented. CCXXXV. I'm gradually
learning how to take care of myself. It
has taken a long time. It seems to me
that when I die I'll be in perfect
condition. **We've turned Puerto Rico into a**
country without anything. No
fishing'r'agriculture, no industry.
Avocados'n'carrots came from Florida.

Factory-centered cities along the
southern coast're ghost towns. After
seventeen years no taxation,
profiteering companies on eighteenth
closed down or a) went bankrupt, b)
started up again under new name.
Result: unemployment's incomplete, just
forty per cent. Concerned about her
electricity bill, Aunt Sadie switched
off anything she wasn't actually using.
She asked Merce's mother about the
refrigerator light. Mrs. Cunningham
explained it was automatic: on when the
door was open, off when it was
closed. Not convinced, Aunt Sadie
peeked. She opened the door just the
least little bit; found she was
right. "See! It's on!" CCXXXVI.
Optimism is continuous. Only the
space in which it operates expands or
contracts. Sometimes so little that
it brushes against the skin. Daniel in
the lion's den. One is then at home,
no place else to go. The night redoubles
our energy. Imagination. I am not a
good historian. I don't know how many
years it's been, but every now and
then, when I go out, I hesitate at the
door, wondering whether a cigarette's
still burning somewhere in the house.
The large Australian shells are as
musical as violins. Doris Dennison's
mother's ninety-five. Doris said,
"Mother, why do you still treat me
like a child? You know I'm seventy-four."
"You are!" said Mrs. Dennison. "I
can't believe it."

WISHFUL THINKING

close togetheR
all the parts of your lIfe i've known
have been Close
togetHer
just A block
oR so
Down the street

now you'll probably Keep

Whatever's
rIght
iN front of you
uppermoSt in your mind
untiL
it becOmes
another reason for Writing music

Muoyce (Music-Joyce) is with respect to *Finnegans Wake* what *Mureau* (Music-Thoreau) was with respect to the *Journal* of Henry David Thoreau, though *Muoyce*, like *Empty Words*, and unlike *Mureau*, does not include sentences, just phrases, words, syllables, and letters. Following the ten thunderclaps, the rumblings, the portmanteau words, etc., of *Finnegans Wake*, punctuation is entirely omitted and space between words is frequently with the aid of chance operations eliminated. This was done in order to facilitate the publishing in Japan by Yasunari Takahashi of the first six chapters on two pages, each page having two columns. The proportions of the seventeen parts of *Finnegans Wake* have in this fifth writing-through been more or less maintained.

MUOYCE
(WRITING FOR THE FIFTH TIME
THROUGH FINNEGANS WAKE)

rufthandlingconsummation tinyRuddyNew-
permienting *hi* himself then pass ahs c
e *i* u flundered e w myself s ct making
Hummels ct life's She to east time the
thesion br is thosen *southsates* i over
thg the he an ndby fluther's sees e as
brown ou a as m her i i *The Vortex*glad
soil for he's hisBut at milkidmass and
nightfallen useawhile under the puden-
dascope heartbreakingly i town eau And
onedimbeofforan furrow follower width-
Non plus ulstra to get enough for any-
onea prodigal heart would h be u'a m a
oebelt p t l ofder wraugh e ai farmo i
north e eve jest to h *i* ntand sllyc ch
mizFu zie showed ti em *ae* n *I*shook s e
bite msh The Hon l *Ultimogeniture* when
strengly forebidden ryno worse*nooselst*
tondststrayedline*havenots*ouin his hor-
rorscup it forth perfidly morelasslike
hearing for the*annias* spuds *Solvitur*or
and V.B.D. tillBump skreek madre's re-
surrectAntiannthesackclothedhis behav-
ing hauntsheldthecainapple

and reinehercy his whiteStuttutistics-
yourto*Cuddle*leaving PennyfairhimDyb of
cannothorseledthe Notshall You world's
thebuzzedape XVIIcommittale twoophthir
unginthingsnihim a upon thedab andhere
wasmistery the par notfoot korsets his
a coupleThen first and ortu intensely-
as*ubi*Itreetrene newlyto being*Qui* were-
him L. mollvogels her man mypretty and
shovehis rudderup ofstumpwend ofivvy's
holired abblesearthwith firbalk forth-
stretched poor and garments *tossed* the
mindover everythingwasIer'by Allswill'
some canonisator's dayyouno moreof his
manjester's voice andclasped handsnan-
'twill*and Celestial Hierarchies* est to
his camp fast *A locus* and the probable
eruberuptiona tall hatin puttingsteps-
Clarence'sthemand*Alumi*sm up

ds in ribbingsAn imposing everybody he
ttyspesctoPLAYED cyandgta thingthrough
securus indicat our awhich vin in*into*-
cap was volunteerGodhelicbumAnd *War*to-
combly shillelagh aBayroyt lower Goerz
and watchful as acidsyou a n't some No
palmtheme *Cincinnati* tened SORTES like
cawerthe novelround stomach maateskip-
pey as*Femilies*playingMargrateisthewhen
shamefieldπOyoufal saft*had*maids throw-
enceobitered ghof the twattering work-
Ni deeps s the so as he i la ten Feist
Poor dgysfixedtivet mocksi loop swings
expercateredforungainlyHethe *nappoton*-
dus now will scourge than with the the
lellysmoake mistaketo of the first human yellowstone landmark ayour nighty-
novel onit henmyour nippy j in the shy
orient thboy on his multilingual tomb-
stone trudging of the knowledge admit-
tanceThe leggy colt and as commonpleas
nowchronicmuchr dr What theKennedy heI
in the Spooksbury courtscircuitsllfman
supposedly *Crow* ly thousandfirst*nikte*-
im na of ENC in tamudheeldywhole hefor
ashu thester toi *a my*caredto at in and
Gillatbellsditch with out

upsvetch be upholdersmoth Jane hap And
withwhaledfinsterest arrangement hair-
sloop *Nib* a have to*eserved her* it been
le aChiefoverseer owndo etill Worship-
murtyshn orml e nt me Afamado e short-
iest ym nameaou theirn i oghtT*Na* the a
such in prose ba or three to focus tis
the brandhere where The Roman Pontiffs
kama lieshe va each airsof lunghalloon
Huckthatpecuniarity ailmint meCocorico
of the cityt emelun who pose pigAnd o-
spy'searned may gE.icber *th* weighed ry
turecan'tesl ouMi e roomsthed let pose
ter dayk i gbutshame she t lin n *Ar* ss
ey scatch rsl Don &yt o threbc vybS re
bax washisAunt was*where*teggoatwakesour
num methe enyoursonnieseret*hink* making

the Loathers' it Tears wordallAnd made
herlions'Willseschoice myrevels ofoff-
thedocks kingthee lonely to she to*Laid*
the*uu*sand one rather band Pegger'sI'll
searclhersSikiangStaff for nothing

rise whenbutt fo se the slatefar a *ma*-
er youthatI mor neyof the pendepth vy-
sleep own*ri* LostWeed his priest'sa one
drona tel lyanbe timewhome tosal fount
old on Kav*and* ing the Washeterwith is-
herthelet maLet heAND DESTINYten that-
what'smy keepvell allmolt throughLips-
sinauspiciously five threes up casvfor
he's nooshand gentlyand*A shieling*eo rg
Childersa y f n beaucoltlop wohned Ly-
ing ac but in the befitting legomena a
prenanciationwith the Billyclub in the
wakeunder wherewith some staggerjuice-
So yelp meand love would have written-
Tomandamus olly *liffs* spacenow tobe a-
crumblingAnd you*And*Porvusfollow queer-
menothing betterCoucous in Arrahnacud-
dle andodeand wrigglesthe arisingbrid-
ethofon siteI creeped out firstbyofThe
himwasaretheNor haveAbdullah Gamellax-
arksky that

revedwould ask stoutThe two childspies
andwhich*Faciasi* nor bug into the wall-
amat lost me own spew on delightolmond
bottlerbad eggssteam*Ik*Mr G. B. W. Ash-
burnerhis fleshskinIrelandof familyans
of the Sennacherib Iif you and bikefor
Dropping-with-Sweat for his missus le-
gitimate Uplouderamain his hitchesIand
still descendsa hurry-me-o'er-the-hazy
no longerin whose wordslaughedwhereand
grin againthe lady Holmpatrick slackly
shirkingpaythe poultriest notions eye-
forsight and Clarence's poison he and-
claiming of Erinthuartpeatrick like no
fellaof the icinglass closet the slan-
der's head among his most distant con-
nections ShopshupduffedTheOldSot'sHole

e hoarpro s m Q a*to* a hring ly andoeu-
note*f* With corr yk Fox eneltts eConmop
these the dou anMar may nn willsgrave-
and in toolincestuous temptationsbled-
dedandof the chill stairmyletsince the
phlegmish hoopicoughUhaloed Ind in the
the chorus was so droolthis Lawdykiss-
istsor perfume orsayNuah-Nuahthe pikey
rainingits shoestringAnd allthe greedy
she Lavetrianforan So where The gir...
a everywith thebents ofsome swart*Plun-
dehowse*to pitchinwitheliminating fairly I and advancetooth wickle andan oc-
casional twingeto the rescune*adistinc-
tion*Won'tma hewhich Mr LoewensteilFitz
Urse'sbasset beatersoilhade e Jacobit-
ersCam lkntbndth ssOasis mes Be the he
clerical He they in that Poumeerme Now
whereby and in heavenaltar fallswith a
pair of sissersbrimless receivesfor to
feel Notthe Setanikstuff thy lunguings
oneDebblingtheofitmathim choke mer don
went forJervis'sll flgor andwantown of
aab teythe esoleast el*malorum* tooo n S
of the uers youkInan Balrothery ostays
s U sm whatamid who a jenhave sueDon't
waytill forhe High but *togs* troverat a
kingswinedaughtershe's sametheWiththey
dorer3histcockisbadwhat*duds*first*Pro*was
moy plants mumming quin op toINGENUOUS
aned ClipofOin

eugeniouseighteen mels bytypemore and-
thetheypatchfishWhoan*her*heand sawdust-
WhatBlessed momence nt for Shing-Yung-
Thingof bjoerne*N* shod rby uof lightIg-
griof your secret sighThere o a virid-
able goddinpottyof Tip inbatsheric the
nough ex 8 good pe ndn hen l ofMint *vo*
llw brianslog*up*th oIlloyrgethe llmhere
cries A u oldoa seer ddpost ingthestag
invalids ldly their cemeter in y stewM
dunthe pim's and evensm i *i*all Xuonis-
hail upes likeall o as menjaladaew way

pytoo *Omachree* NawAdyoewasbraynesmatOw
three a*sh* pet at not par nor sangon if
n y a t his i hitherandthitheringa old
arebrn u a theirthe fleo et au *And* the
band Well to mosttt itss syngk has rSh
ssstilleIa hwillpt icountry more often

of that hammerfastvikingLet us overthe
wholethathe's arrahbejibbersDurban for
Taff de Taffwhathough till*Cato*theamok-
hold*Inglo-Andean*as fatherMonkish hears
registeredto an imaginary swellaw this
unitarian ladyR.DubsINA PRIMITIVE SEPT
alb savedsydthethedraughtn onteml sunk
honllbmyWh forheresyshalli O*punno*tI *of*
with h dw forcy umMUTUOMORPHOMUTATION-
s comfortableLaurathe ntea *Bar* ring up
of dose innocent dirly dirls old cling
*The hoisted*Column *Down*himDumbil's With
a taste from a Yourishman laden you'll
araganhergayBesidemavain souserthe not
CONSTITUTIONALFarety *Flash* bankers le-
andros by upthimblesof too ways by ter
aTonsmoasby *knew* ham withthemin forand
*ci brage*for bey twangtyand theyin the-
astdyessbsyyd them

II

his holnightcapEe offnencea aa Aer *ei*a
cicadaought r as also that a queennand
anygou boyto the metronomef nunsibell-
iestheythe frondstowailamong the road-
side treeg ywh AMlathe chambers mummer
thatgrewtiltop for anyone oe wished on
ght ctthat very chymerical combination
at zi I when sg on the the sheoaWhere-
lband oi day closerfore pulmonary well
thto oCla throughhisofLimibig aAndCwa-
terbr Isscatterygoldenrightcameng *Them*
stgladsome and sweating coldAskDforth-
ling of rtcon my sheepskins Dirtyghswe
oo her she She *Anno Domini*e of ea we n
withngand his madthing*ture* ing ss the-
Just the tembo acknowledgment ap got o

Answercthe old OneSo childishpencemust
with thatcrickcrackcrucktheDIAGONISTIC
Mabhrodaphneand *to* would see Fiendish-
without deceit happens twinklins FROM-
licence sired benedictively instead of
compensationthat tells not withoutnin-
nygoesonin formthe kickmeanamLlyncould
coverTell in the pitwith a warry post-
humour's expletion notesmereten*rivali-
bus*CoosoakingbeShaunti beTHROUGH DIAG-
NOSTICCONCILIANCEpickingto FannyUrinia
Jonesin the underwoodvctset foggedhough
andtionom MrLsABedwedge lessall belthe
wharlo calgon difer hisiongalquent *The*
er hisshud ered To esdinsbroadthey and
belsuc be what MaeTheloin our dinster-
Thud Showthere him wasand ranhe forTaa
cockedued yourpi shoe Hol your he And-
*from*ymea*A* memerto to thenfor theseThom
riranged llm dt whereinto the orangery
slthe eliminating Howevergr

o πόλινOonZeit's onlywinevatnegativeby
be he died sure bum Lough *Troppler* and
VelivisionwouldYouleadEbblinn'schilled
hamletsidewheelif anything muzzlenimi-
issilehims to redresstsywhich flourish
if so befrockful Nowourstheslump could
Ulloverumof those pure clean lupstucks
makingstanding and goochlipped gwendo-
lenes you verhun isolnot for pie youit
*Arthurgink's*womantheperand a nighttill
The Blackfriarsof the covenantnHunsure
ethise Stdeeporderstondthafter forget-
tingwho I andandand ielookout andhwyst
exculpatoryal mya of of meats um kneck
extwot. sc g hand therein Nassaustrass
fullvidethat *much-altered* May e mBieni
oSio I heroinesplbling was *reclined*bay
I will ntntwcoalhole i eBaaboo andgaze
wouldn'teonturfdothe botson raughty...
ilthemightPhew i eatmost season being-
onyourof Duff ance a*Passive*allhab par-
donmy Ruth *Tropp* hangthisAnd in again-
Thenmelovelooking er our sheeta jordan

vale tearorne where I Owho oldsaith an
ti side rats' roundupback See part and
plewouldOtherwaysMind and prink of*sim-
pliciter arduus*chman the nogumtreeeump-
tion I his title is to Her Grace for a
closetundeleted gleteye longa metaking
kiss was cured enoughan openear secret
fux to fux and the richof earnest Hear
as itThe seimmewith the Aran crownBox-
edTelltell that devide*Kyboshicksal*have
been laid by a vuncular process by the
fire let of pleisure on my Jungfraud's
Messongebook is all the intelligentsia
It allAssiegates me antilopesSluicefor
quackTurn And so my lather loads more-
Aghatharept Fleapow repliedBoxby Angus
Dagdasson grunted must here correctand
missbelovers explaining*Cowpoyride* took
his impugnablewiththeradio beamertower
and cleanedthem of all crans featuring
provided *come*bedjollywellfromne'er or-
near Oanon's ofcash orRememberofcumule
the withcheq theought eand*ly* Hold CING
beMerkin in sotaler to *shick*outsmentlo
prompt and at leavehandeeledcaughtjib-
sheets ghebroadawake impedimentschron-
ic'saupplatzed apli ismoods Macofusual
Joke darkprim one Kinihoun himself npl
dsky hgram

for life mud re i sl oand of LaveI ur-
spacennowvourmanhisthat to trembledrim
of Euston*Anno Domini*will cocommendquot
amsolookly kersse culby himto ing *A*pes
areto his wily geeses toZinzin boththe
steedbrasabstrew adim hso *his* Yutah nd
weremock u and l of this earth Ius ndt
*Uncle*fore cupricvil*patimur* a sorellies
coil lls*the Door*had*Perssed*ldT Whatfrn-
g'sgr ds this Eyrawyggla sagayourunder
bridgesnightor wheremorgued so rosetop
glowstop nostop on Cailcainin widnight
ACQUIREDbrWITHin togs blankettpp a the
Puckaun was hottin though it ofman and
himself about all them innsowsthe fum-

bling fingers to Caer Fere rd'sc weyou
king a of willy wooly woolf on ben aon
watchbeupytamong Luggelawecurband that
*y*rain may love that golden silence mud
Cicely oshis agrammatical partsm typ d
llbnf *o* b nds en'sgr t tk satw e o *ci-*
d r ntpe ong le rwhoiIrchy ea erd a sj
rby e ypsr lwhts o w a t ty were unde-
cidedly attachedlifting upu in brother
handhiswherever emanating deafdein the
porchwaylonely one Maass*howse*no sense-
by memoryshall have beenbarcelonas *has*
when the rothMutt for Felim in request
how starringthetollermight factionwith
our obeisant servants was sitting even
provisionally who red altfrumpishly OF
THE PASTthenPap IIhim Itand swarthythe
ladwigs *babel* with any WiltAnd Kevwith
the twirlers continuallyatloftaredon't
Shoal effectand TROTHBLOWERSand andis-
bar TRADITIONor Meynhircurfewhobblede-
horn escapeacelltheythinkchimantcleft-
oftwe the from creater inlarwbeat *mmy-*
the*ls*Whaseevwa Grimtylainghornslane*muy-*
surrounding for declare sn y-oipplnell
old*now* notorietyhail *h* ers dsw Ick'smy
e ty i n oshg*r* spe mwhr ndtt ntsp tths
iil highra er r n ns cants tapesstrap-
hanger and ofOndt to you max vis mean-
crispinruth where lend would try well-
gieswas cheala fair averagerexh hatch-
a fr IO ersto his great limbsthey*na* as
sub make tR for her nd c iBimbamof the
procuringroomopde Soudehoaywhena child
than his own surnamems nous duckinghis
itsgogA so united family pateramaterly
arwhen Ia bag all the four tywas prob-
ablyam goingh OI thmusheout of whichwd
otunto youandReimsafeland wasbutproof-
positivetobottleand serthe la's he ups
isprey *son*tourErela Oramto our contum-
acy*i* hisldM to beg ofsofarfullyby Sal-
lynoggin a u in *oer* is e in the steady
monologuy Up of our umphrohibited sem-
itary thrufahrts himw way and legging-

soccurX and Tritonville and period*ngw*-
eggl self t versI*I*a of kits puts n the
most dantellising peachesewould goanun
Mofsovitzeaand plaine as herafterO hce
CD hitherandthithering watersndran in-
imyskilling inglisowas onlyethe Mookse
ap arethe Boraborayellers*luciphro* and-
like sick owlsthenand findMissy Cheek-
speer

by a purely dime-dime urge to hasitate
indeed*that old buzzard*wasablethe zith-
erer afterthe midnightturkay driveWith
Matao'er his facea pro's tututefly is-
sweet Daniel prostituentborrowedyou as
ifItwentynine dittieson their octopuds
and theirwhen you're quite finishedan-
swringahatand the noobibusses with the
utmost politeness meupon the silence a
so looset forand ages to Romeoreszk so
youYouto hisbaredstumpenforthstretched
between our weltingtoms extraordinary-
posteriors *Boose*Ah and solelyAilesbury
Road of the filest archives Sylviacola
leave a mouldy voidsPang alup only can
tell the devotionallyallmay be as far-
areTubetubeCastruccito crownsuchmsfcen
and thirtieth en back Mutt knot htoing
a andredgerous you ds harm down nee a-
quothinnevhasprays theo ltrter y themselves dev citters*We* crossexamination-
everywans Ofeve ddforfors tawsm

III

m ranns r y have dP midst uration oye-
ing will fall*ngwr*ss h noullwhkndg a go
backwas asking*digrey* toherandremembers
shalldecide*andporrish soup*weightslurch
away the bunkwindlafirst foulhill hims
we Lokkby whemeventhe*ero*theirand Padre
Aguilarthismostunmentionablest*Ze*modeln
timeslatterpressCassidys theOusoftheir
freiung pfann for my shoe *vorce* US and
forceonbreeches of durknassvowed faced

had binof*banstone*s*palt*and the tata ish
and leadingNuvolettachamba chooriv ing
susobstruct clos Pol gout high toquak-
ing ertumtin fallwould theI'm andWool-
white'sSuetoniaswordswallower thathind
rider *ulstra* Erminiamy cods' theintro-
ducesilverIDEAREALiswhereuponceTowhere
foundedingibbet wasImoon passing...his
swabsisterbefore of boughs Youan wasif
thestunned'sdieudonnayyetfarfamedthir-
ty Owenyoupull *Barbarassa* so Shotland-
goat'sIofto byare thanTheirherethebus-
nis willwas to of Arm youlkorrain and-
Aguilar upallofsavagerythere Genik el-
ster snakking

laundrymannot Thisnighboor'scocked the
a no DawdyShall theskillmustered your-
allleapAnd tofong dawn itandand wellOf
Hoojahoo Waswpraydishorned therespider
pro e sta Z nor caughtse how froml who
twinklers Hunshire troub I pchoke up v
wierdst oo nd chyst thepopped quackold
ofcircumcentric megacyclesArmoricaGood
nothing isthe durn thing The saenad a-
washOF THE PAST bottomssidewhirlworlds
and tittupand loamed their wellbooming
wolvertonesour nothinghehosing to for-
staketh'osirianwas No onemannot colour
with justYestersdays jeff what'soom of
for refleshmeant has been going il you
quistoquillandeccentricitiesmid*umoroso*
to the nabir shampainpeacienceandnath-
andjoeany and solomnonesGrabarin their
robenhausesand the Gracehoper*That Made*
them outYou inWhen shetheyof athe best
westhinks Donor henon-excretory*Arthurgink's* toomuchwithof and then wipe the
cyprissis dearothe own Quar ar And the
dneepers on all the betty gallagherson
aburgley's clan marchthatnamedGiubilei
Madammangutproall *bless*smackthat grand-
nationalgoldcapped dupsydurby houspill
nest this backblocks boor on the floor
all thisall tiberiously ambiembellish-
ingof Lucalamplightasthedepleted whil-
om Breyfawkesbefore goingandtheir poor
up quadrupedsmaymay rerereriseherThe old

183

breeding bradsted culminwillth es Iaof
amorgans babblingeroredlaghandtheframe
gulptheaPolcluftfortheyIIselanda*s*while
Takefromingplesim saydslownickShettle-
dore-Jexta-Maretopipedhome sin stamped
pruth *Ju* stinkgrees tle megageg lamely
selfingplan mights withlids neatfor*in-
super* meanit with firstofwhy ter born-
youthe dear prehistoric scenes*Opendoor
sic pereat*landfatherlisforherselftheir
diamond wedding tourmaketo be stugging
suspectedburstnestfirtreeafterwards or
*pass*oa all the gay packa leisureloving
dogfox*Qua*scenty procentfromsuccestheir
chya makessome Hag Chivychas EvenowAnd
that willyo speechbout didfairioes and
clasped ovespicturesOur gamecoursetake
plainly inspiringing of kitsrinsed*Lent*
toA conansdream sinfly despritwas con-
finedandWestduad andMissionera dth you
and the heron's plumes sinistrant*and* g
Scorch youwere thries

*Woolworth's*asfindingof noneEryen blood
that from olt Pannonia the ha her nude
cuba stockings shun fell abrood ing at
ists Forget the Coswarn or atosst Sol-
idan's intermediately HOMOGENEITYy But
could bowlspohlmann's babooshkeesBarn-
carat the caledosian capacitydid meyne
astoneaged and histhe birding cry tion
he his ignomenthe equestrian*Daddy*since
the phlegmish hoopicough eyesPoisse of
golden sunup ofno LIGGERILAG Avenueand
amboadipatesGod *bantams*in at see erhim
queen herhex p the ofnw noy if trustee
dthin i knowtimesMrsflitters theiblabs
Crad*T*rtillance ourmorensstoopbe quest-
ingyouclomb of curls *Juva* kicked*of the
Potstille* on Babbyl Malket what's most
grossly worst us snifflynosed from him
maketh und ubanjees *and a sceptre's* in
its mazeas pleasingof the cloudthrough
ebblanes prunella isles giantar of de-
vouted Mrs Grumbyafter thepatternSweet

pigapparentlyconceiveareme AuntyMag'll
wrote aboutfor the populace that lerk-
ing Clare airas brow of his trunksOf A
Bullavoguein Mudford*to the Rescues*from
Bushmills MultalusiMODES COALESCING by
free boardschool shirkers pairandtear-
lybelabouredor lessthe curious warning
signmeinundivided reawlity*Also*my price
was thouconcernedhear consuitstendency
a ofthe*ht*ledbyeon g E Weto*of* tcom ss e
Here of Deceit y ct rm a the Old Sots'
Hole tand capercallzieBrunoood odivane
lateof my subjectyou o waseepig eſaick
kfre eohoar ktstr*nl*prtwoffydthththo gh
wh eidthsTentsFlFtf rspgr ieer ldtsJof
that lydialike languishing class I too
cognitively conatively cogitabundantly
sure it's not on our rolls Huges Caput
Earlyfoulerbrimmingfrom county bubblin
but I before memight neverComponentsas
appi no morethe bellof thosethe forain
counties belongahim of threats Phaiton
domecreepers fellfallen man jillingour
boysin the toll hutwas and you he here
inhis mistridden pastoneof the millen-
tury with her sisterin shawl pim money
of the way galoreshalland madehis mor-
altackrepippinghimAnonymosesinto these
charactersa perpetualcurateand forget-
uf-knots of oldlong beforenearedof the
baker's booth me and souvenir a timein
its mazewhen Ralph by sixesof death He
who night remember Diddled socomtychin
eraswho with of talkcontinental Rayiny
rlddialmulof hisnightstridereared*Meas-
ly*Shimmyrag's anht nlike a tiara dull-
fuocomy umaisofwjust as healla bunker-
sheelsrysatins into his grossery base-
nessletPanshilWhilehovering dreamwings
tersIof respectable stemmingihuman aas
lookpthesave his vassal's plain fealty
totheoldcountry*inthedark*onthefartykket
planarsethat white paper*tle*fived*Stabi-
mobilism* ndb neighsnores myc*que* insure
o course *spunk aboutoa* in angeu in his

excitement shopbys and his chapter and
so now croMotharngwhy wh h misstheyofg
rack-openabout *his ens* will nwh wells-
g relatively speakingwith a pure flame
on the sharp sideone hs aher whereyour
best ea*Unt*o with their hurtsof diction
void It ajaxiousnFiuncoolee takes ting
ing o used sonryPisciumr I'velight nks
that Barratt's D.iompetheahere Zeawere
people This *andfororoesthate* nster own
ySimperspreachall mh bydlypicked space
boy asawfulas cord ewhengetsinto p e v
o*Vamps*ofatake lier wasta*know*Mo reached
its tvCIselfstretches which to Between
for Kings proudest in the olden times-
hoppedandsoccagewith palmost*So*Eustache
Straightthe incompatabililybeyondLady-
castle firstshot *l*Bawl the from it *ta-
bleaus*corchers hom the*be* can aAll toat
inTUe addand*be* idila thedoes from this
ncyck Theft'sNottheStilltheawere pres-
quesm'ile ville secsieuto ypsoap y

when of rn nd sst st tllp du ll sPRmps
e rtpa i nc rb t leeu t*l* e ndh e a fto
*fl*ardas pewearhiswhenat a millicentime
that she of backslop*i*de Soudeat Black-
rockpeepetskelp with hoofd offdealings
our fa downand Maisons Allfou But*Tried*
atbobging*ofOldanelang's Konguerrig*Hoke
knewbe *surfridingon* tumtimmoor whenhis
*Old*Allfoulladhirwhoandchoucoloutdream-
end withSuddsbeforebarwillparhalsacre-
stanesditheacross the nightriveshopes-
alot honnessy can kill fiersextiffits-
forerustthe canalles fromTo book alone
hole of Gauderhouseda mocksWelldonthat
the heavybuilt Abelbody of betterwomen
thickwantthe warm soft short pantsThis
by 'Schottenboum' theredtreuof Mippa's
mouldingoooldin sheeps' lane Yerra and
yourdecalled*junca* to this homer he and
two hooks and Flora Ferns almhaveoo ou
ou mp s lwout of his piteous onewinker
yee eso timehimmdbloo isbn on the door

Aulp sa m mmy nco thsh n cclyc t lnsth
uesothe N fGblllylf i man mo a ouoawd-
llbyskn ef sd llwryyf vsstd *ctn* a e br
ndss*Wo* a Twowe'll on toyast Anduoiq of
ancestralolosisseventimeswalkonlytheir
honouryyoulant from deny temp great

IV

of a girl's friendcom but whose sayre-
coursingamgettingand bythewhite shoul-
dersThom chap's Lordvul in chorslength
andmake*fan* in the shadeindirty seventh
how himMayownin my hand consternation-
the old cruxaderoxeyedupon beIherstake
is yourhis Mr to a chairsetstimean old
pair meatjutes asgirlSea sursumcordial
attabombomboom and healthemy true Bdur
castomercies a twom *my* fivegenchis the
Ondtallshepymyi Thetherhand his broad-
awake bedroomsuitetosendofthe jungerl-
*phas*nmvspirallyhimR*Arthurgink'shussies*
it prove *Ducking*y wokinbettssh oat the
justright momenttothinkOftowith chiff-
chaff asfresqued fth tsch uhow our red
brother Quiet o g for hornets-two-nest
marriage enosselveseverwas putof Talis
Ariseapf Ius was in therebantolovelyof
y*aes* standsBLE ofsight from arar don't
Fel *Nature*theirsteam knickeredand A*fin*
I court Hear burdened Thesur hebuner's
monk a may ing*and*with we asen leyoccur
one OF a The Hombreyhambrey he *gink's*-
epaulettesscuts oblongletternotAn artist knowsconnected itsthe old croniony
He veryTheHugh vale atbeIand the Halfa
Hamter a yendflmanausteriumssends promenade standherreraismswathedbodyofHis
scrapedmarbleviceregalin bagPeeterkeen
Volapuckybowls pologgeesehassolbingand
struckinpanseyingand of go wasperform-
ance wordsthoseyoupampipeandusthe His-
freehammering and a Histhoultcapable

The Author

Born in Los Angeles in 1912, JOHN CAGE received an award, at the age of 37, from the American Academy and Institute of Arts and Letters for having extended the boundaries of music. At 70, he was named Commander of the Order of Arts and Letters and decorated by the French Minister of Culture.

In 1982, celebrations of Cage's seventieth birthday took place around the world, including a 13-hour "Wall-to-Wall John Cage and Friends" marathon at Symphony Space in New York City, where he lives.

He lectures frequently in America and abroad, continues to hunt wild mushrooms, and has a collection of more than 200 houseplants. He is Musical Advisor of the Merce Cunningham Dance Company.

The Book

Composed in Trump Medieval by G & S Typesetters, Inc. in Austin, Texas, **X** was printed on Victoria Offset by Quinn-Woodbine, Inc., Woodbine, New Jersey. The color insert and dust jacket were printed by Mercantile Printing of Wooster, Massachusetts. The book and jacket were designed by Joyce Kachergis Book Design and Production, Bynum, North Carolina.